THE WILD GOOSE CIRCUS

a play with music in two acts concerning the story of a dysfunctional circus

Russell Davis

BROADWAY PLAY PUBLISHING INC
New York
www.broadwayplaypub.com
info@broadwayplaypub.com

THE WILD GOOSE CIRCUS
© Copyright 2020 Russell Davis

Cover art by Hanna Moors

First published by B P P I in 2004 in an earlier version in *Plays By Russell Davis, Volume 2*
This edition: August 2020
I S B N: 978-0-88145-803-9

Book design: Marie Donovan
Page make-up: Adobe InDesign
Typeface: Palatino

THE WILD GOOSE CIRCUS was commissioned by the New York Theater Workshop through a New York Council on the Arts commission grant. It had readings and development work at NYTW; Sundance Institute Playwrights Lab., Utah; New Dramatists, NYC; Playwrights Theatre of New Jersey, Madison, NJ; the Public Theater, NYC; New York Stage & Film, Vassar College, NY; Juniata College, Huntingdon, PA; Virginia Tech. University, Blacksburg, VA; University of Puget Sound, Tacoma, WA.

THE WILD GOOSE CIRCUS was produced by the Annex Theatre, Seattle, Washington, opening on 8 June 1995. The cast and creative contributors were:

JOSHUA KARABOS .... Michael Shapiro
PETERLOO .... Sara O'Neill-Kohl
CLOTILDE (JILLY) BEAN .... Kathie Horejsi
KOMODO LILY .... Alicia Roper
LALA BELJANSKY .... James B Chestnutt
POLLY BLODGETT .... Susanna Burney
NICOLA (NIKKI) JUNOD .... Alicia Roper
PASQUALE .... Sara O'Neill-Kohl
DARK SHAPES or BEASTS ... Cathy Sutherland, Doug Fahl,
Bruce Hall

Director .... Mark Lutwak
Scenic & lighting designer .... Tobin Alexandra-Young
Costume designer .... Cathy Doherty
Properties designer .... Stephen Weihs
Mask designer .... Margaret Doherty
Composer .... Robin Holcomb
Sound designer .... Wier Harman
Production stage manager .... Julie Vadnais

CHARACTERS

JOSHUA KARABOS, *a ringmaster*
PETERLOO, *a clown, or vagabond*
CLOTILDE, (JILLY) BEAN, *a high wire lady, also known as*
  CLOISONNE
TILGERTOONA-TIGLATH TILY, *an acrobat and disguise*
  artist mostly referred to as TOONA TILY
LALA BELJANSKY, *a juggler*
POLLY BLODGETT, *an equestrienne*
a BEAR, *(played mostly by* TOONA TILY*)*
NICOLA (NIKKI) JUNOD, *a fortuneteller*
PASQUALE, *a child who disappeared*
certain DARK SHAPES, BEASTS *or* VISIONS *that loom in the*
  background

SETTING

A one-ring travelling circus.

A freestanding pole, like a ship's mast, is upstage center. Across this pole is rigged a torn banner, or curtain, perhaps seven feet high, and ten feet wide, which drops to the ground.

A few long strips, or torn sheets, of canvas are stretched along the edges of the stage and into the air above. Like the remains of a tent.

To one side is an overturned cannon.

Downstage is a trapeze, but hanging close to the ground like a swing.

Up above, but not by much, is a tight wire.

Time: Probably the present.

PLAYWRIGHT'S NOTE

There is mention of a bear and unicycle and tightrope and the advent, also, maybe of a parade. But none of that has to be literal. Or maybe some of it does. This play is about what we might choose to imagine, or believe. And how that might determine who we are. Meanwhile, things should be simple. There are scraps of fabric, the remains of a tent, through which we can see the sky or some other world beyond. And for all the allusions in this script to Samuel Beckett, or W B Yeats, or the prophets Elijah or Isaiah, it is essentially a clown act. That's all. A tale of yearning.

Just six actors (4F, 2M) are needed for the nine speaking roles in this script, including the Bear. The ensemble may or may not be augmented by several individuals with circus and movement skills.

Finally, the punctuation in this script may seem unusual at times. It is not meant to indicate, however, in any way how the lines of dialogue are to be phrased or delivered. It's really about the thoughts, the specific shifts of feeling or insight, and such things can be halting or run together. It's the actor who, according to her or his own dynamic, finds the focus or momentum in those various moments.

The playwright thanks John O'Hagan, director and fellow clown, and Hanna Moors for their insight and presence during the further development of the script.

ACT ONE

Prologue

(Soft, incomplete music.)

(The stage is empty.)

(Upstage, behind perhaps a scrim, the shadow or silhouette appears of a young clown running from one wing to the other. She is pursued by another silhouette holding aloft a scythe.)

(The stage is empty again.)

(Enter JOSHUA KARABOS *upstage.)*

(He wears a faded coat and dark breeches. He regards the torn banner and overturned cannon. He comes downstage. He regards the audience.)

JOSHUA: *(To audience)* Pretty still, yes? This stillness, for a circus.

(He listens.)

Hardly even any music.

(Pause)

(To audience) There should be a parade right now, don't you think? Some trumpet sound. A loud proclamation. A big bang to shake us up. And this music, it should be pushy music. Exaggerate. There should be people here. Exuberant, happy people, shouting and singing: Hi, Hello, We Are Happy, You Are Happy. And in this circle you should see a pretty lady riding by on

a leopard. A bear traipsing, yes, with a cow. Lions
should play before your very eyes. People should eat
fire. We should have clowns and jugglers. I should
stamp and blow a whistle: We are the best, the first, the
greatest! From territory untouched by the colonial past!
We come to you from across the dark ether! To present
forms of life that can live only briefly, like a revelation,
on this earth! We have come to fight the netherworld,
do battle for you, with beasts from the end of this
world.

Yes, of course.

I must claim these things. Attack your intelligence.
What you think cannot be true.

(Pause)

But we are not that kind of circus. No. Not so boastful.

*(PETERLOO, wearing a red nose, and out of breath, enters
from the wings. She holds a silver whistle. She approaches
JOSHUA, but then heads furtively instead for the torn banner
upstage. She disappears behind it.)*

(JOSHUA doesn't notice.)

JOSHUA: *(To audience)* Once upon a time maybe we
were. A little boastful. But something happened. Yes.
On our way here, it was terrible. Caused a dysfunction.
I'm afraid so. The exact nature of this dysfunction I
cannot say right now. When it was, or how it came
to be. Some fire, perhaps. A big wind, they say, or
earthquake.

*(PETERLOO peers out from behind the banner. She
approaches downstage, holding out a whistle for JOSHUA.)*

JOSHUA: *(Continuing to audience)* Or maybe just a
subterfuge, it was some malevolence or malignancy,
this dysfunction all along. There are many opinions, in
our circus, about this dysfunction.

(A DARK SHAPE *appears from the wings, along with a floating balloon.* PETERLOO *sees the* DARK SHAPE. *It pops the balloon.* PETERLOO *flees offstage. The* DARK SHAPE *chases after.)*

(The banner flutters, then billows.)

*(*JOSHUA *turns upstage.)*

*(*PETERLOO *and* DARK SHAPE *are gone.)*

JOSHUA: *(To audience)* For now, you must simply know we have lost some of our tricks. We are not the circus we used to be. We are scattered. Like a ship which is washed up. We are coming ashore to you. In bits and pieces, like remnants, of what went before.

*(*CLOTILDE JILLY BEAN *enters from the wings, dressed like a tattered ballerina. Her tights are patched, and she holds a parasol with a rip in it. She drifts upstage, disappearing behind the banner.)*

*(*JOSHUA *doesn't notice.)*

JOSHUA: *(To audience)* And so we will have a hard time to show you the circus. We are going to have to show from what is left. What we can recall. And if we come to a place we cannot do, like our horseman, Elias, he could ride a chariot through the air with horses on fire. And our magician. She could take up a sword in her hand and a plowshare instead would appear. Or a spear, it would vanish into a pruning hook. And our parade also. Which was led by a child. This child could make the sundial go backwards. Make the spring and flowers reappear in your eyes. And when our child spoke you could see rivers flow back upwards into a mountain. You could hear the foothills sing. And those horses. We had a host of horse riders, all of us, beautiful, like standing in the sun. With words in our mouths shining like a sword.

(CLOTILDE *has entered again the other side of the banner.*
She drifts toward the overturned cannon. She touches one
of its upended wheels and turns it. She turns it again, as if
steering or piloting some craft.)

JOSHUA: *(To audience)* When we come to that, those
parts, which are very pretty, we will have to stop. And
explain them to you.

(CLOTILDE *picks up a broken balloon from off the ground.*
She pays no attention to the audience.)

(JOSHUA *turns. He regards* CLOTILDE.)

(CLOTILDE *sits on the trapeze.*)

JOSHUA: *(To audience)* In the beginning, I was going to
tell you there was a parade. We began with a parade,
like a ripple, on the face of the deep. But as you can see
Clotilde is here. She is ahead of schedule. And who can
know the next time she will show up, if I do not talk
with her now?

(Soft, incomplete music stops.)

JOSHUA: Besides for me, in my heart, our circus can
always begin, like this, with Clotilde.

First Scene

(JOSHUA *goes to* CLOTILDE. *He takes her by the hand and*
leads her downstage.)

JOSHUA: How do you do, Clotilde?

CLOTILDE: I am fine.

JOSHUA: Good.

CLOTILDE: Very fine. Thank you.

JOSHUA: Nothing wrong today?

CLOTILDE: Nothing, no.

JOSHUA: How is the music today?

CLOTILDE: Pardon?

JOSHUA: *(To audience)* She hears music. A band in her head. Everyday a special band tune. It is wonderful.

CLOTILDE: I do what?

JOSHUA: The band. All the music, the mandolin, in your head.

CLOTILDE: I do not.

JOSHUA: Yes, strings. A flute. It's an old-fashioned band. You told me.

CLOTILDE: I never hear a band.

JOSHUA: Today is different?

CLOTILDE: I never hear a thing in my head. My head is boring.

JOSHUA: I do not think so.

CLOTILDE: Poof. I have nothing in my head.

JOSHUA: No. You told me yesterday. You hummed to me.

CLOTILDE: I did not hum. I cannot hum.

JOSHUA: You hummed the band tune.

CLOTILDE: I am too busy to hum.

JOSHUA: Oh, yes?

CLOTILDE: I am looking for a ship.

JOSHUA: *(To audience)* I love when she is busy.

CLOTILDE: A ship. Which is on the horizon. It is going to take me away.

JOSHUA: You are going away in a ship?

CLOTILDE: Yes. I am departing soon.

JOSHUA: I did not know this.

CLOTILDE: Oh, yes. It is too boring in my head here.

JOSHUA: And who belongs this ship?

CLOTILDE: It's a pirate.

JOSHUA: Ah. *(To audience)* She is busy seeing a pirate.

CLOTILDE: Did you see him? The pirate?

JOSHUA: No, I did not. There is no pirate today.

CLOTILDE: I'm sorry.

JOSHUA: It's okay. Do you remember my name?

CLOTILDE: Yes. I do.

JOSHUA: Can you tell me?

CLOTILDE: Yes, I can.

JOSHUA: Well, go on. Tell me.

CLOTILDE: Okay. You are Lala Pastelly.

JOSHUA: Who?

CLOTILDE: Pasqually?

JOSHUA: No. No, Lala Beljansky is a juggler. And Pasquelle, she was a child. We have lost her.

CLOTILDE: Oh. Okay.

JOSHUA: You do not remember these things?

JOSHUA: Then you are Tooting.

JOSHUA: What?

CLOTILDE: Tooting?

JOSHUA: No. Mr. Abaddon Tooting is dead. You don't remember Mr. Tooting is dead?

CLOTILDE: No. I'm sorry.

JOSHUA: He is dead. *(To audience)* This is Clotilde. Clotilde Jilly Bean. She walks the wire for us.

CLOTILDE: He can't be dead. I saw him.

JOSHUA: You cannot see Mr. Tooting, Clotilde.

CLOTILDE: No, I saw him. I saw his clipboard.

JOSHUA: *(To audience)* Clotilde escaped as a child from a place called Bloomfield. She could see pirates in this Bloomfield. Calling to her, outside the windows, to come for adventure.

CLOTILDE: *(To audience)* This man is mad because I thought he was Tooting.

JOSHUA: *(To audience)* And she could hear music. Even then. The band I have told.

CLOTILDE: *(To audience)* I agree. This cannot be Mr. Tooting.

JOSHUA: *(To audience)* And so in her mind she would wander. She would roam, looking for where this music can come from. This call to the high seas. Until finally she came to us.

CLOTILDE: *(To audience)* Do you know this man's name?

JOSHUA: *(To audience)* She became our special act. See the wire up there? She is like an angel now. On a balcony, yes. To another world.

CLOTILDE: *(Swatting* JOSHUA *in the arm with her parasol)* Now I remember!

JOSHUA: Ummph?

CLOTILDE: You are not Mr Tooting at all.

JOSHUA: I know this.

CLOTILDE: You are Caravelle.

JOSHUA: Pardon?

CLOTILDE: Carabella?

JOSHUA: My name is Karabos.

CLOTILDE: Oop. Sorry.

JOSHUA: Joshua Karabos.

CLOTILDE: I am sorry. You are the man in charge. The boss.

JOSHUA: *(Pleased)* I am the ringmaster, yes.

CLOTILDE: I remember now. I had it confused. Mr Tooting is looking for you.

JOSHUA: Mr Tooting?

CLOTILDE: I'm afraid so.

JOSHUA: He can't be looking.

CLOTILDE: Yes, he's looking. He told me. He pointed to your name on a clipboard.

JOSHUA: Clotilde. There is no more clipboard.

CLOTILDE: Oh, yes. He has a list to read from the clipboard.

JOSHUA: Clotilde, this is very bad, this relationship you have with a person who is dead.

CLOTILDE: *(To audience)* This man, I'm sorry, our ringmaker, he is blind. He can see only to the edge of his nose. He has no periphery.

JOSHUA: No periphery, Clotilde?

CLOTILDE: *(To audience)* Including Mr Tooting.

JOSHUA: *(To audience)* I must apologize to you sometimes, I'm sorry, for Clotilde.

CLOTILDE: Don't believe me. I don't care.

JOSHUA: *(To audience)* Mr Tooting was in charge of all the animal acts. He was nasty at his job. He liked to poke in the ears, and the eyes, of the animals with a sickle. A scythe. To make them pay attention. The elephants also, they could come out at any time and chase me.

CLOTILDE: They were not elephants. It was a bear.

JOSHUA: Pardon, Clotilde?

CLOTILDE: You are mistaken, Carabellum. You are thinking of a bear.

(PETERLOO *enters upstage, still holding a whistle. She tiptoes toward the torn banner. She disappears behind it.*)

(*A* DARK SHAPE *appears followed by a balloon. The balloon pops.*)

(JOSHUA *turns upstage. He sees nothing.*)

CLOTILDE: (*To audience*) This man was chased by a bear. Which bit him and ate him up. He was aten.

JOSHUA: I was aten?

CLOTILDE: All up, yes. Mr. Tooting has told me.

JOSHUA: (*To audience*) It's okay. She will join us soon.

CLOTILDE: (*To audience*) He can't remember. He is afraid from when he was aten.

JOSHUA: (*To audience*) It is the dysfunction I have mentioned. When she talks like this.

CLOTILDE: (*To audience*) Oou-ah. I hate when he uses these words. This dysfunction.

JOSHUA: Clotilde, I have explained this word many times. Over and over.

CLOTILDE: Don't shout at me.

JOSHUA: I am not shouting. You don't remember how you nodded your head?

CLOTILDE: I always nod my head. To keep you happy.

JOSHUA: I am happy. Thank you.

CLOTILDE: No, I am afraid if you fall over.

JOSHUA: What?

CLOTILDE: You fall boom. Have a blackout.

JOSHUA: I do not fall boom.

CLOTILDE: *(To audience)* This man is a fainting man. Pah.

JOSHUA: No, you are speaking now of the dark shapes.

CLOTILDE: *(To audience)* No adventure, no poop-la, in this man.

JOSHUA: You have seen these shapes. You told me.

CLOTILDE: *(To audience)* Ooou-ah, my head is boring here. Like an island. I am marooned.
(She drifts off to the side.)

(JOSHUA watches CLOTILDE, benevolently.)

JOSHUA: *(To audience)* She has forgotten how we talked. How the dark shapes, they sneak up. Like a mist from behind. A fog to lose our memory. I'm sorry. She forgets the past. Mixes elephants with a bear. You never know which world Clotilde can walk in. It is hard to synchronize.

(CLOTILDE sits on the trapeze. She gazes out front. She quietly hums to herself.)

JOSHUA: *(his voice changed)* But I will hold off these dark shapes. Watch out for you. Like a sentinel, with a lamp, in the night. I will be your watchman on the tower. You warrior upon the high seas. So we can get through this circus show, poof, boom, before they arrive to take me away again.

CLOTILDE: What did you hum?

JOSHUA: Hm?

CLOTILDE: I heard you humming.

JOSHUA: No. I did not hum. You heard a humming?

CLOTILDE: *(Getting off trapeze)* Like a ship. A voice on a ship.

JOSHUA: What?

CLOTILDE: Could be someone on a ship who hummed.

JOSHUA: Ah. I did not see this ship.

(CLOTILDE *goes to the foot of the pole supporting the wire. She places her hands and feet on the bottom rungs. She climbs.*)

(JOSHUA *is excited.*)

JOSHUA: *(To audience)* I think this humming she has heard, it is the band again. I love how this can happen. Come back in her eyes. All the hoping, the expectation. Like the beginning again, the very beginning, when all the world was good.

(CLOTILDE *stands at the top of the pole. She steps out. She slowly crosses the wire.*)

(*Music. A soft ensemble with flute and strings.*)

JOSHUA: *(Enrapt)* Ah. There she is. My little lady. Who walks the wire and forgets the past. That's how she walks. To forget the past. She hears music. A little band in her head. I hear it too. Every step she takes, every bounce, I hear a mandolin. A little harp in her head. A flute.

(*A strain of something malignant, discordant, begins to seep into the ensemble music.*)

(CLOTILDE, *becoming apprehensive, turns back and heads for the top of the pole.*)

(*Several* DARK SHAPES *appear in the wings.*)

(PETERLOO *pops her head around the side of the banner. She puts the whistle to her mouth. She tries to blow it.*)

JOSHUA: *(Continuing to audience)* That's why I'm here. In case she forgets. Or if she's scared. I can hum it. I can sing it back to her.
(*He hums.*)

(CLOTILDE *climbs back down the pole.*)

(PETERLOO *runs around the banner, silently pointing at* DARK SHAPES.)

JOSHUA: *(To audience)* I can sing until she's safely across. Till she makes the other side.

(Exit CLOTILDE *into a wing.)*

(Exit PETERLOO *into the other wing, chased by* DARK SHAPES.)*

(The music stops.)

Parade Scene

*"Turning and turning in the widening gyre
The falcon cannot hear the falconer;..."*
Yeats, *The Second Coming*

(The sound of many marching boots, like an approaching army.)

(Enter TILGERTOONA-TIGLATH TILY *[*TOONA TILY*] in whiteface from the wings. She wears an oversized top hat, an outsized coat and black boots, which are ridiculously too large for her. She marches downstage, circling past* JOSHUA, *still to the sound of a host of marching boots. She drags a large canvas bag behind her. From the opening of the bag protrudes the blade of a long scythe.)*

*(*JOSHUA *watches, somewhat immobilized or nonplussed.)*

*(*TOONA TILY *comes to a halt. The sound of marching boots stops. She takes off the top hat and swats* JOSHUA *in the elbow with it.)*

JOSHUA: *(To audience)* Excuse me a moment.

*(*JOSHUA *turns to* TOONA TILY.*)*

JOSHUA: Hello, Toona Tily. How are you today?

TOONA TILY: Okay.
(She nods. She salutes.)

JOSHUA: *(To audience)* This is Tilgertoona-Tiglath Tily.
She is our ancient Assyrian acrobat and disguise artist.
She would like us to think she comes from a place out
of time. Where all our laws of chronology do not apply.
This is so, Toona Tily?

TOONA TILY: Okay.
(She wiggles affirmatively in her boots.)

JOSHUA: *(To audience)* It is claimed by some that
Tilgertoona-Tiglath Tily is descended all the way
across the millennia from Tiglath-pileser III. The man
who restored the Neo-Assyrian Empire which caused
also the destruction of the northern kingdom of Israel.

*(TOONA TILY steps out of her big boots. She leaves them
standing beside JOSHUA. She tiptoes toward the banner
upstage.)*

(She looks behind the banner.)

JOSHUA: *(Continuing to audience)* Her native tongue is
said to be the Neo-Assyrian dialect of Akkadian. What
they spoke in cuneiform on those clay tablets. And so
she is not, I'm sorry, too good sometimes in how we
speak our own language.

*(TOONA TILY tiptoes back downstage. She steps back into
her boots. She smirks.)*

JOSHUA: You are early, I think, Toona Tily. Ahead of
schedule.

TOONA TILY: Yes, thank you.

JOSHUA: Did you see Peterloo? She has gone, Peterloo,
to fetch my whistle.

TOONA TILY: No whistle, oh, boy.

JOSHUA: We can parade, it's okay. With no whistle.

TOONA TILY: Parade, goody!
(She begins to march jubilantly around JOSHUA.)

(The sound of many marching boots.)

JOSHUA: Please, Toona Tily, please! *(Stepping in the path of* TOONA TILY*)* These boots you wear are much too loud.
(To audience) You must excuse Toona Tily. She is excited. She is the chief person in our parade. She likes to dress up. Take the place of all the people who are missing. Including also the animals.
Yes, Toona Tily, this is true?

TOONA TILY: *(To audience)* Yes, thank you.

JOSHUA: But you must not bring a bag like this on the stage.

TOONA TILY: No bag?

JOSHUA: No. You must keep it behind the curtain. No one is going to steal. Go on, take it away. I cannot introduce a bag.

(TOONA TILY *pushes the canvas bag a foot or so upstage.)*

JOSHUA: *(To audience)* She has costumes from all over the worldwide. She drags them in a bag. To be ready, in case of a parade.

(TOONA TILY *slaps* JOSHUA *in the elbow with the top hat.)*

JOSHUA: What is it, Toona Tily?

(TOONA TILY *whispers in* JOSHUA*'s ear.)*

JOSHUA: Ah. *(To audience)* She wants me to tell you this is not the color of her face. This is whiteface. *(To* TOONA TILY*)* They know this.

(TOONA TILY *whispers again.)*

JOSHUA: *(To audience)* Ah, yes. She cannot show you the color of her skin, her true spots, because all her face, it was hurt in the dysfunction.

(TOONA TILY *steps out of her boots and tiptoes upstage to the canvas bag. She opens it and digs inside.)*

JOSHUA: *(To audience)* But as you can see, it is a very pretty face. Smooth. Like the ocean moon. She was in fact the Lady in Our Kissing Booth. She was very good, Toona Tily, for business.

(TOONA TILY slips back into her boots downstage. She holds a picture in a frame. She slaps JOSHUA in the elbow with it.)

JOSHUA: Toona Tily, please. It is not good to bang like this in the elbow.

(TOONA TILY hands JOSHUA the picture.)

JOSHUA: Yes. *(To audience)* This is Toona Tily in the kissing booth. Probably you cannot see from so far in a picture. But Toona Tily has also some posters, very big these posters, all in the kissing booth.

TOONA TILY: *(Starting offstage)* Posters, yum yum.

JOSHUA: No, Toona Tily, it is not time now to show posters.

TOONA TILY: No posters? *(To audience)* Sorry.

JOSHUA: We must put away now this picture. Also this hat. You cannot wear a hat like this.

TOONA TILY: *(Tipping hat)* Pretty hat.

JOSHUA: *(Realizing)* Ah. I see you have Mr. Tooting's hat.

TOONA TILY: *(To audience)* Pretty girl in a hat. Kitty cat.

JOSHUA: No, this is much too big for you, Toona Tily. You are tiny, like a rabbit, in this hat.

TOONA TILY: No touching.

JOSHUA: And what is on the legs?

TOONA TILY: Boots.

JOSHUA: Yes, they are big for you, these boots. *(To audience)* I think this was the Mr Tooting Clotilde has seen. He was big, the Tooting. Like a monster in these boots.

(TOONA TILY *pulls a clipboard out of her overcoat. She is about to swat* JOSHUA *in the elbow, but he intercepts her.*)

JOSHUA: *(Taking the clipboard)* Yes? What is this? *(Reading)* "A note to ringmaster Joshua Karabos from Nicola Junod our fortuneteller."
(To TOONA TILY*)* This is a note to me from Nikki Junod?

(TOONA TILY *wiggles affirmatively in her boots. She salutes.*)

JOSHUA: *(Reading)* "I have Mr Tooting in my tent. He wants to meet you. Presto. He has things on his mind to add to our list."
(To TOONA TILY*)* I cannot accept this note. It is stupid.

TOONA TILY: *(To audience)* Sorry.

JOSHUA: Since when did you take notes from a fortuneteller?

TOONA TILY: *(To audience)* Sorry. Stupid note.

JOSHUA: *(To audience)* I must apologize to you, I'm sorry, about this Tooting.
(He goes to the overturned cannon. He tosses the clipboard down the mouth of the cannon.)

(TOONA TILY *steps out of her boots. She tiptoes back upstage.*)

(PETERLOO *appears, tiptoeing backwards from one of the wings. She turns and sees* TOONA TILY. *She flees around the banner.* TOONA TILY *grabs the scythe out of the canvas bag and gives chase.* PETERLOO *escapes into the wings.*)

JOSHUA: *(To audience)* This Mr Tooting liked to make a list. A list to foretell what could go wrong in our circus. Like a big wind to blow the tent down. An earthquake also or a fire which broke out.

(JOSHUA turns and sees the canvas bag still onstage. TOONA TILY hides the scythe behind her back.)

JOSHUA: *(Sternly)* Toona Tily, you must take away this bag. I have told you, no, to the bag. This hat too. Take away all this Tooting. We must make now a parade.

TOONA TILY: Oh, yum yum. Parade, goody.

JOSHUA: Yes, goody. So quick to the wings. Go rouse Lala. Polly Blodgett too. And tell Peterloo, tell her to forget my whistle.

(TOONA TILY marches jubilantly around JOSHUA to the sound of many marching boots.)

TOONA TILY: Parade! Parade!

JOSHUA: That's right. That's the way to rouse.

TOONA TILY: Everybody! Parade, parade!
(She marches upstage waving Mr. Tooting's hat and shouting:)
Parade, parade! No touching! Parade!

(TOONA TILY sticks the handle of the scythe into the ground upstage. A DARK SHAPE appears and hands her a sign. She hangs the sign on the blade of the scythe. She exits into the wings.)

(The sound of marching boots stops.)

JOSHUA: *(To audience)* Toona Tily likes when I tell her to bring the parade. To rouse them.

(Enter PETERLOO from the other wing. She slips unnoticed behind the banner.)

JOSHUA: *(Noticing the canvas bag)* Oh, no. Toona Tily! Toona Tily! You have left the bag!
(He goes to the bag.)
(To audience) I'm sorry. It is no good. A bag like this on the stage. The parade could trip.
(He drags the bag to one side of the banner.)

(Enter PETERLOO *from the banner's other side. She sees the sign on the scythe* TOONA TILY *stuck in the ground. She disappears behind the banner just as* JOSHUA *reappears.)*

JOSHUA: *(To audience)* I think I have just seen Peterloo. She is hiding again from the circus.
(He looks behind the banner.)

*(*PETERLOO *pops out front again. She slips behind the banner just as* JOSHUA *comes out again.)*

JOSHUA: *(To audience)* Ah, yes. It is Peterloo. She is always playing like this. *(Turning to banner)* Peterloo. I know you are there. I know we can play peeky-peeky-poo. But did you find my whistle?
I asked you to fetch the whistle, yes?

(The sound of an uncertain whistle from behind the banner.)

JOSHUA: *(To audience)* She has found my whistle. I can tell.
(To banner) Peterloo. What else did you find? Besides the whistle? Did you find this singularity theorem you tried once to tell me about. The quantum-relativistic possibility that all time, even space, could disappear?

(No response)

*(*JOSHUA *notices the sign on the scythe. He peers at it.)*

JOSHUA: *(Reading)* "Turning and turning in the widening gyre..."
(Smiling at audience) I'm sorry. She is bashful. Peterloo cannot see the same world which we can see. She sees a monster. Hears sounds. An invisible big mouth which can chase and chew her alive. Break her apart into quarks and gluons. Make particle physics out her.
(He peers at the sign again.)
(Reading) "The falcon cannot hear the falconer."
(He takes the sign off the scythe. He goes to the cannon and stuffs it down the cannon's mouth.)

(Meanwhile, TOONA TILY *enters upstage, tiptoeing without her boots. She pushes a large poster picture which moves on caster wheels. The picture is of* TOONA TILY *in the kissing booth. She heads for the banner which starts to billow and flutter.)*

*(*PETERLOO *steps out from behind the banner, pointing frantically.)*

JOSHUA: *(To audience)* And so she is always afraid. Pointing always to look. But when I look, I can see nothing.

*(*JOSHUA *turns to see* PETERLOO *still frantically pointing.* TOONA TILY, *however, has slipped behind the banner, which is now still.)*

JOSHUA: *(To audience)* Perhaps it is some hole to the next universe. Or some big crunch. This singularity theorem she sees. Which will swallow us.

*(*TOONA TILY *emerges from behind the banner. She grabs the scythe.* PETERLOO *flees. They run around the billowing banner and disappear into the wings.)*

*(*JOSHUA *doesn't notice.)*

JOSHUA: *(To audience)* Or perhaps just a hallucination. A foreboding, I don't know. Because if she could speak, then she would tell me, like Cassandra, what is on her mind.
I must explain also she does not always know you are here. And Peterloo is not alone in this dysfunction. I too can forget there is an audience. Under certain pressure. Lala and Polly, they also forget.

(Enter PETERLOO *upstage pursued by* TOONA TILY. DARK SHAPES *appear and tackle* PETERLOO. *Everybody rolls behind the banner. The banner shakes.)*

(The sound of thumping and banging.)

(A large, heavy cloth is thrown onstage from behind the banner.)

JOSHUA: *(To audience)* Ah. Peterloo has found something for us.
(He goes to the cloth and picks it up.)
It is a flag, I think. Hmm. With skull and bones.
(Sternly) Peterloo. Who gave this to you? Who gave the Jolly Roger?

(The sound of thumping and banging.)

JOSHUA: *(To audience)* She seems very busy, Peterloo, in her mind today. We have no pirate act in this circus.

(A large book is thrown onstage.)

JOSHUA: Ah. A book.
(He goes and picks it up. He opens it.)
(Peering at first page) "THE BOOK OF GRAVES. An intelligent man's guide to the Bottomless Pit." *(Turning page)* "By Abaddon Tooting."
(Sternly to banner) Are you reading this book? Did the fortuneteller give this book?

(PETERLOO emerges from behind the banner chased by DARK SHAPES. TOONA TILY, who now has the whistle, follows, wielding the scythe. They circle the billowing banner and exit into the wings.)

JOSHUA: Hm. *(To audience)* Toona Tily is trying to capture Peterloo. Probably for the parade. I am sorry about Toona Tily. She is gone strange. Since these notes from a fortuneteller.
(He takes the book and flag. He stuffs them down the mouth of the cannon.)
(To audience) But we cannot worry about Nicola. If our fortuneteller is restless. Because we must have this parade. The parade must go on.

(Music. The sound of an ethereal parade.)

(The stage goes dark. Lights focus on JOSHUA.*)*

JOSHUA: Yes. Because I remember the first parade I
ever saw. It was right here, in this circus, when I was
a child. I remember because I waited in the darkness.
Trying to be still. To hold the wildness back in my
imagination. Be calm. Like the face of the deep. When
out of the dark came a voice. It spoke a word in
here. Like a trumpet sound. And up jumped all the
lights. And in this light, I saw a whole parade. With
many creatures in sight. I could see a bear. Playing
with a cow. And I thought, this is funny. How can
a bear play like this with a cow? And then I saw a
lion, and in the company of the lion was an ox. And
then I saw leopards. Many dark leopards, with billy
goats following. There was a wolf too. And in and
out, between the legs of this wolf, came parading a
lamb. I was astonished. All these creatures together,
happy together in one parade, every creeping thing.
And leading the parade, I was even more astonished.
Because I could see a child. A child was leading. And
in the eyes of the child I could hear a strange and
wonderful sound. I could see the mountains and hills,
they were singing. I could hear trees clapping their
hands. And the feet of this child, they were beautiful.
And I could hear a voice say to myself, a small quiet
voice, causing a stillness in my mind, it said: You have
to be in this parade. This parade is for you. Where a
child can lead in a parade like this.

*(*DARK SHAPES *come up behind* JOSHUA. *They throw a
large, empty canvas bag over his head and pull him to the
ground.)*

(A brief snatch of music. Then nothing)

(Blackout)

The Bear Parade

"Things have changed since yesterday."
Beckett, *Waiting For Godot*

(Lights come up.)

*(*LALA BELJANSKY *and* POLLY BLODGETT *stand in front of the banner on either side. They look out front.)*

(A scythe is stuck in the ground. A sign hangs from the blade with new words in quotation marks.)

(Downstage is a large, empty canvas bag.)

(Pause)

*(*LALA *notices* POLLY.*)*

LALA: Do you know where this is?

POLLY: Hm?

LALA: This place. Can you tell me? This flat lonesome spot.

POLLY: I'm sorry, no, I don't know.

LALA: Hmm.

(Pause)

*(*LALA *and* POLLY *remain looking out front, as if waiting for a bus.)*

LALA: I thought perhaps there is a parade.

POLLY: Hm?

LALA: A parade maybe. I heard about it. In the past.

POLLY: Oh, really?

LALA: You heard about it?

POLLY: A parade?

LALA: Yeah. When it's coming. It's gonna come this way?

POLLY: I suppose.

LALA: I think so too. It's gonna pass right by us.

POLLY: Well, good, then.

(Pause)

LALA: Ask me if I had a sleep.

POLLY: Pardon?

LALA: We can talk about sleep. Until this parade.

POLLY: Oh. Did you sleep then?

LALA: Yeah, pretty good. I had a sleep in a ditch.

POLLY: Ah.

LALA: Yeah, I was giving chase, I think. To a bouncing ball. I think this ball belonged once upon a time to what I was doing.

POLLY: Hmm.

LALA: But then this ball came to a ditch, it bounced over, like a bunny rabbit. And I didn't see the ditch till I fell in.

POLLY: I'm sorry.

LALA: It's okay. It's a restful place to sleep, this ditch.
(Pause)
How about you? Did you sleep?

POLLY: No. No, I don't sleep. I see horses.

LALA: No kidding?

POLLY: Yes. Big dark ones. When I close my eyes. They come at me. In some sort of stampede.

LALA: That's bad.

POLLY: Yes. I find it safer out here. Out in the open. Where there are no dark horses.

(Pause)

LALA: You sound British. I like the British.

POLLY: They're sweet, yes.

LALA: They are good eggs.

POLLY: You sound East European.

LALA: My name is Lala. Beljansky. You heard of me?

POLLY: No, sorry. I don't believe so.

LALA: Then who are you?

POLLY: Blodgett. Polly Blodgett.

LALA: Yeah? I knew a Blodgett once. She rode on horses, I think. That's not you? On the horses?

POLLY: No, I told you. They stampede at me.

LALA: Hmm. Then it must be somebody else. Yeah, riding these dark horses.
(Pause)
What do you think happened to the parade? This one we have mentioned?

POLLY: Perhaps it's late. Unless of course we're late.

LALA: They had the parade?

POLLY: I imagine.

LALA: Hmm. I thought somebody, I was sure they roused me. *(He notices the scythe stuck in the ground. He steps to one side to read the sign hanging from it.)*
It says here things have changed.

POLLY: That's nice.

LALA: Yeah, since yesterday. Do you see a change?

POLLY: No. No, I hadn't noticed.

LALA: Good. I guess then we can expect a change.
(He regards the banner. He regards the overturned cannon to the side. He turns front again.)

(The distant moo of a cow is heard.)

LALA: You know. I can remember once a parade.

POLLY: It's coming back to me too. Was there a child? I seem to remember a child.

LALA: Yeah. He was in front, I think.

POLLY: Yes. And wasn't there a bear?

LALA: Ah, yeah. He was mischievous, that bear.

POLLY: And do you remember the cow? He was friendly with the bear. They played together.

LALA: I don't remember this cow.

POLLY: Or was it an elephant?

LALA: No, I remember seals. Seven seals which came at the end. Along with some horses.

POLLY: What horses?

LALA: There were four dark horses.

POLLY: No, I remember only one. And that was white. With some fellow riding. Quite lovely, he was. With those words in his mouth, all shining like a sword.

LALA: Hmm. Maybe this is not the same parade.

POLLY: That could be. Because I can't remember any seals. Unless, of course, you're confusing an elephant with a seal.

LALA: How can I confuse an elephant with a seal?

POLLY: Well, they're both gray.

LALA: No. One is big. It has tusks and four feet. The other is little. Like a tadpole.

POLLY: Then you must have seen a walrus. A walrus which has tusks, that's what you thought the elephant was.

LALA: No. What possible parade could have a walrus?

POLLY: Well, obviously our parades are different. They've been different all along.

LALA: I think so too. But at least we can know one thing. There was a bear. We both saw a bear.

POLLY: Precisely. And a child too.

LALA: Good. So maybe it's the same parade. In the beginning. It's the ending, that's all.

POLLY: Yes, of course. The ending's all different.

LALA: I think these parades, your parade, my parade, they parted company. Splitted up sometime.

(A brief sound in the air.)

(A DARK SHAPE appears from behind the banner. It grabs the scythe and disappears again.)

LALA: Did you hear that?

POLLY: Yes. I believe I did.

LALA: Sounds maybe like music.

POLLY: Awfully brief, don't you think, for music?

(A burst of carrousel music. A loud whistle)

(Enter a BEAR from behind the banner S L. The BEAR wears a top hat and has one large boot on. He has a silver whistle hanging from his neck and holds a scythe. Hanging from the blade of this scythe, at one end of a rope, and dangling by its neck is the mannequin or doll of a CHILD tied to a clipboard. A DARK SHAPE follows behind holding the head of a COW, which is mounted, like taxidermy, on a piece of plywood. The BEAR, CHILD and COW circle downstage. The BEAR trips over the canvas bag. He kicks it aside.)

(LALA & POLLY watch.)

(The BEAR, CHILD and COW circle back upstage and exit S R behind the banner.)

(Carrousel music ceases.)

(A balloon pops. There is a brief flutter in the banner.)

POLLY: I wonder. Could this be the parade, you suppose?

LALA: That's not any parade. Which I remember.

POLLY: No. And that's not the child.

LALA: Yeah, he looks phony, that child.

(Carrousel music)

(Enter the BEAR again from behind the banner S L. Over each paw the BEAR has now a hand puppet of a SEAL. The SEALS are tossing a white ball back and forth between them. A DARK SHAPE follows wearing the mask of a LAMB. BEAR, SEALS and LAMB circle downstage. The BEAR slips on the canvas bag. The white ball goes bouncing off into the S R wing.)

(A balloon pops. The music stops.)

POLLY: Is that a second bear? Or the same bear, do you think?

LALA: Is that the ball I was chasing?

POLLY: Really, that ball?

LALA: It's white, yeah. Same kind of bounce. Like a bunny rabbit.

(The DARK SHAPE helps the BEAR back to his feet. BEAR and SEALS pick up the canvas bag.)

(Carrousel music)

(The BEAR tosses the bag from SEAL to SEAL. BEAR, SEALS and LAMB circle upstage. They exit behind the banner S R.)

(Music stops. Banner flutters.)

POLLY: Yes, I'm rather certain now. This is meant, I'm sure, as a parade.

LALA: This is a parade? One lousy bear?

POLLY: Well, no. Wasn't there a cow?

LALA: It's missing its body, that cow.

POLLY: Then perhaps there's more on the way. Perhaps the bear ran on ahead.

LALA: You got to be kidding.

POLLY: No, I've seen worse. I'm sure it'll get better.

(An explosion offstage)

(The banner shakes and billows. One large boot, one top hat and one SEAL hand puppet fly out over the banner.)

(LALA and POLLY dive for the ground.)

(Meanwhile, upstage, the POSTER PICTURE OF TOONA TILY glides out from behind the banner. It rolls toward the S R wing. Enter the BEAR giving chase, with one SEAL still attached. The BEAR wrestles the PICTURE OF TOONA TILY to the ground and drags it back behind the banner.)

(A white ball comes bouncing on U S R. The ball bounces behind the banner and then out the S L wing.)

(Pause)

POLLY: I think we better talk to him.

LALA: Yeah. He's having some trouble back there.

POLLY: You should speak, I think, to that bear.

LALA: I can't be seen talking to a bear.

POLLY: You should ask if there's some sort of meaning.

LALA: What, to this parade?

POLLY: Just ask. Ask the meaning next time he comes around.

LALA: No. I cannot ask meaning from a bear.

(Carrousel music strikes up again. A loud whistle)

(LALA and POLLY scramble to their feet.)

(Enter the BEAR with one SEAL from behind the banner S L. The mouth of the BEAR is trying to get the SEAL off his paw.

A DARK SHAPE *follows wearing the mask of a* LEOPARD.
The BEAR, SEAL *and* LEOPARD *circle downstage.)*

POLLY: Ask him. Now's the time to ask. Wave at him.
Make him stop.

LALA: I cannot stop this bear. He's eating lunch.

POLLY: You want to watch this forever?

LALA: This is forever, you think?

*(*LALA *steps out in front of the* BEAR, SEAL *and* LEOPARD.
The BEAR, *etc slips and gets tangled in the ropes of the low
hanging trapeze.)*

*(*LALA *and* BEAR, *etc regard each other. Music stops.)*

LALA: Excuse me. Who are you the person inside this
bear?

(No response)

POLLY: Try a leopard.

LALA: He's looking blank at me.

POLLY: Maybe he wants you to call him a leopard.

LALA: I can't call something like this a leopard.

POLLY: Then ask about the parade. If it's on its way.

LALA: Oh, yeah. *(To* BEAR, *etc)* Excuse me. Can you tell
me which way please is the parade?

(The BEAR *frees himself from the trapeze ropes. He pushes*
LALA *into the trapeze.)*

(Exit BEAR, SEAL *and* LEOPARD *behind the banner S R.)*

POLLY: I knew you should have called him a leopard.

(A balloon pops. The banner flutters. LALA *frees himself
from the trapeze.)*

(Enter the BEAR, SEAL *and* LEOPARD *from behind banner
S L dragging and pushing something in a large canvas bag.
They leave the bag downstage.)*

(The BEAR *regards* LALA *dusting himself off. The* BEAR *pushes* LALA *backwards over the canvas bag. The* DARK SHAPE *takes off the* LEOPARD *mask and places it on* LALA.*)*

(Exit the BEAR *into the wings, still with a* SEAL *on one paw. The* DARK SHAPE *follows.)*

POLLY: You seem to be getting in his way.

LALA: *(Taking off mask)* Maybe we should look in this bag. Which is kicking.

POLLY: I'd rather not.

LALA: You have something better maybe to do?

POLLY: Well, actually, yes. I was watching a parade.

LALA: Nah, it's never gonna end, this crazy bear.

POLLY: Perhaps if we were to join in. If we participated.

LALA: What? With ourselves?

POLLY: Yes, in the parade. Instead of standing outside, being smug, you know. Critical. I mean, what other parade is there?

LALA: I could rather think I have missed it.

POLLY: But perhaps it would look better, this parade, if we were actually in it.

LALA: I could rather wait for what will never come.

POLLY: No, I think we should look at it from that perspective. From the inside. We should make that sort of gesture. We should go out, and join that cow.

LALA: Shut up about the cow.

POLLY: I think this is what all the cavorting has been.

LALA: What cavorting?

POLLY: Pushing you over like that. And the costumes. The music. It's been an invitation to join in.

(Loud crash offstage. A dog barks.)

(Chase music)

(Enter BEAR *and* SEAL *chased by a* PIRATE FLAG *draped over somebody, like a ghost.* BEAR, SEAL *and* PIRATE FLAG *circle downstage.* LALA *flees.* BEAR, SEAL, FLAG *and* LALA *circle back upstage and disappear S R behind the banner.)*

*(*POLLY *watches.)*

(Enter the FLAG *S L of the banner and enter* LALA *holding the head of a* COW. *They circle downstage. Enter the* BEAR *on a unicycle giving chase. He hurls the* SEAL *off his paw.* LALA *and* COW *get tangled in the trapeze and fall over.)*

(Exit FLAG *into the wings chased by* BEAR *on a unicycle.)*

(Chase music and dog barking stop.)

POLLY: Was it fun, then? Joining in?

LALA: A white horse is back there.

POLLY: Pardon?

LALA: Yeah, it's lying alone. On the ground.

POLLY: A white horse, really?

LALA: I think so.

POLLY: Quick. Let's see.

*(*POLLY *exits behind the banner.* LALA *follows.)*

(Soft strains of music, like a lullaby.)

*(*POLLY *and* LALA *reappear S L of the banner. They hold the front and back legs of a* WHITE HORSE, *which has a brightly colored carrousel pole through its torso.)*

LALA: I don't think this can stand by itself.

POLLY: Yes. Well, at least it's white.

LALA: Let's put it back.

POLLY: No, I think it wants to graze out here.

LALA: Nah. Somebody else can take care of it now.

POLLY: No. We should parade. Go for a parade with it.

LALA: You're crazy.

POLLY: Yes. I think I can hear music.

LALA: Yeah?

POLLY: Much sweeter music, yes. Than before.

LALA: Yeah. You can keep track of the tune now.

POLLY: Good, then. Let's parade.

(POLLY *leads* LALA *and* WHITE HORSE *as they circle downstage. They are oblivious of the canvas bag which begins to kick and move vigorously.*)

LALA: I can't parade with a horse like this. It's not even parade music.

POLLY: Don't be so stuffy. Think of it as a dance. There's a dancing horse between us.

LALA: Where are we going now with this dancing horse?

POLLY: Who cares? Come along.

(POLLY, LALA *and* WHITE HORSE *circle back upstage.*)

(*A white ball comes bouncing on from the wings. It disappears behind the banner.*)

POLLY: Oh, look! It's your ball. It must be going too.

LALA: My ball is going where?

POLLY: To the parade, you silly.

LALA: Yeah, where is this parade?

POLLY: Come quick. I believe it's behind the curtain.

(POLLY, LALA *and* WHITE HORSE *exit behind the banner S R.*)

(*The canvas bag onstage struggles and surges. It begins to break open.*)

(*Music swells.*)

(Enter POLLY, LALA *and* WHITE HORSE *from behind the banner S L.* LALA *proudly holds a white ball. They circle downstage.)*

LALA: I think you are right. This looks better from here. This is quite a parade.

POLLY: I'm so glad you agree.

*(*LALA *and* POLLY *notice the* SEAL *puppets and the* COW's *head lying about the stage.)*

LALA: I can see even seals. They are lovely, the seals.

POLLY: Oh, yes, lovely. And look. A cow.

LALA: I'm so happy we found this cow.

*(*JOSHUA's *head pops out from the opening of the canvas bag. His mouth is gagged.)*

*(*POLLY, LALA *and* WHITE HORSE *circle back upstage past the leopard mask on the ground.)*

*(*JOSHUA *looks aghast. He struggles to get their attention.)*

LALA: And can you see the leopard?

POLLY: Yes. Yes, I do.

LALA: He wants to cavort, this leopard, I think, with the cow.

(A DARK SHAPE *appears, holding a scythe. Hanging from the blade of the scythe is a rope, at the end of which dangles the mannequin of a* CHILD *tied to a clipboard.)*

POLLY: Yes. And what's that? Is that a child?

LALA: Yeah. I think he's a child.

POLLY: Good. We should follow that child.

LALA: Yeah. Let's follow him.

*(*POLLY, LALA *and* WHITE HORSE *follow the clipboard. They exit, heading into the wings. The* DARK SHAPE *and* CHILD *disappear.)*

(Music stops.)

*(*JOSHUA *looks bleakly at the audience.)*

A Fortune Tale

(Enter NICOLA JUNOD. *She wears a brightly colored gypsy dress with carrousel figures along its wide bottom hem.)*

(She goes downstage past JOSHUA, *who is still in the bag, gagged.)*

NICOLA: *(To audience)* Awfully still, isn't it?
Once again, so still.
(Pause)
(Smirking) Hardly even any music.
(Pause)
Hello.
I feel so bold, I do. Standing before you like this, wishing to speak.
But the moment has come, I think, to introduce myself.
Nikki. Nicola Junod. Your fortuneteller.
They say I don't know who my father was. He could have been our strongman who married my mother. Or some horseback rider. Perhaps a charming, affluent patron of some sort. Or one of the tent riggers, who knows? But I do know they called my mother a Phoenician princess. They called her Jezebelle. She was our sorcerer. A bewitcher. Who could command any man she wanted in this world. They would bring her gifts. They would bring poetry. They would bring songs to sing to her, sometimes night after night. They all worked so mightily just to foist upon her a mere, bare particle of the intoxication one look from her, or some fleeting touch, could inflict and brew in them. Except for Tooting. The man in charge of the animal acts.

That's the man my mother really loved. The one she
could go for to the end of the earth.
Because Tooting was her phoenix. A chameleon.
Whose body, whose thoughts, never stayed the same.
He shifted like the wind. The ocean beneath. And
whatever he touched could burst into fiery blossom,
or vanish. Be gone. Except for his thighs. He had these
slow moving thighs. And his gaze. Like the sun. Blank
and pitiless.

(She pirouettes. Her dress lifts and floats as she spins.)

*(Intermittent music. The sound of something discordant, or
tiptoeing, in the air.)*

NICOLA: Yes, I'm the child of all that. The girl which
came later.

(She regards JOSHUA.)

This is our ringmaster.

*(NICOLA picks up the LEOPARD mask and SEAL puppets.
She puts them behind the banner.)*

NICOLA: *(To audience)* When I think of a ringmaster,
I think of the British Empire. A little nation of men
that happened, once upon a time, to be just slightly
ahead of everyone else. When these revolutions came.
The First Industrial one, then a Second one. And this
caused something strange to happen. A little nation to
dominate and influence our world.

When I think of the circus, I think of the nation of
India. There are big tigers in us, huge elephants, and
hordes of hungry natives, and violently conflicting
faiths. The ground itself has earthquakes and droughts,
wind, fire, and on the sea I see cyclones.

Now I ask you. For how long would you expect, really,
the nation of India to put up with the little island
of Britain from far across the world? Or a circus to
remain, would you expect, within the confines of what
a ringmaster might expect it to be?

(She regards JOSHUA.*)*

(To audience) When I think of a ringmaster, I also think
of Isaac Newton. His mechanical laws of physics. How
that physics ruled the world. For 300 years. With a
belief in a world that could be measured. All the way
down to its tiniest dot or particle. And then came
relativity. Quantum mechanics. The perception: what
world is there, if it shifts like this under the impact
of our own conceptions? How can we measure, if we
ourselves are the measure? What could we possibly
measure, if there are dimensions underneath? Huge
dimensional presences beneath our tiny decisions to
measure?

*(*NICOLA *picks up the* COW. *She puts it behind the banner.)*

NICOLA: I think the time of ringmasters is over. Yes.
*(She tidies up the stage. She empties the mouth of the
cannon, taking out the pirate flag, book, sign and clipboard.
She places them behind the banner.)*
Haven't you yourself noticed? How this ringmaster
fails to see what goes on beneath his very nose?
He can't see the shift in the wind. How the sea has
changed. Doesn't know it's time now, Darling, to
voyage to a new mental landscape. Time now for a
different voice. A new scout to take us up ahead. To
what we've never seen before. Adventures we've never
yet to have.
Yes. We need a fortuneteller.
*(She takes a false beard out of her pocket. Then a large
colored bandanna and black eyepatch.)*
(To JOSHUA*)* You should not mislead these people. And
say Tooting is gone. Tooting is never gone, I have told
you. He is like the ocean current. What moves beneath
us. What can drown us. And sometimes he can even
surface, waiting, in my tent. With a little list he wants
to read to you.

(NICOLA *puts the beard on* JOSHUA. *She ties the bandanna around the top of his head and places the eyepatch over one eye.)*

(She regards her work.)

NICOLA: *(Patting* JOSHUA *on the head)* You silly goose.
(She pirouettes. Her dress lifts and floats.)
(She exits upstage.)

(JOSHUA *looks dumbly after* NICOLA.)

(Intermittent music ceases.)

(A balloon pops. The banner flutters.)

Pirate Act

(A soft sound. Like a brief band tune. It stops.)

(CLOTILDE *looks onstage from a wing. She sees the bandanna on* JOSHUA's *head.)*

CLOTILDE: *(Softly)* Ooo-la-la.
(She cautiously approaches. She comes to a stop.)
Oh. There you are.

JOSHUA: Mmm.

CLOTILDE: *(To audience)* He is here. The pirate.

JOSHUA: MmmmhMM.

CLOTILDE: *(To audience)* He has come back to me. My pirate. From across the high seas. He has come ashore again.

JOSHUA: MMmm. MmmhHH.

CLOTILDE: *(To audience)* And look. He is sad now. Hear his sadness. His enemies have captured him again. In this bag. They are very evil, these captors. I must set him free.
(She takes the gag out of JOSHUA's *mouth.)*

Hello, how are you, my pirate?

JOSHUA: I am not the pirate.

CLOTILDE: Oh, yes, you are. I can tell.

JOSHUA: Clotilde, help.

CLOTILDE: *(To audience)* I am so happy.

JOSHUA: Help me, please. From this bag.

CLOTILDE: No. I will not help.

JOSHUA: Pardon?

CLOTILDE: You will betray again. I know it.

JOSHUA: How can I betray?

CLOTILDE: You will take your beard off.

JOSHUA: Clotilde, it is not my beard.

CLOTILDE: *(To audience)* See? He will betray.

JOSHUA: I am not the pirate.

CLOTILDE: Then I cannot let you from this bag. You will stay in the bag.

JOSHUA: Clotilde.

CLOTILDE: Until you say again, yes, you are my pirate.

JOSHUA: No. I am a ringmaster.

CLOTILDE: I'm sorry. I cannot hear.

JOSHUA: Clotilde.

CLOTILDE: *(To audience)* I have been looking all day for this pirate.

JOSHUA: There is nowhere to look. There is not a pirate. Not any pirate ship. Even the high sea, poof, the time of pirates, it is gone.

CLOTILDE: *(To audience)* He has become an intellectual, this pirate. I'm sorry.

JOSHUA: No. There is only a ringmaster.

CLOTILDE: *(To audience)* Do you know this word, ringmaster?

JOSHUA: Clotilde, do you wish me to die? In this bag?

CLOTILDE: I will feed you.

JOSHUA: Clotilde, I beg. My duty is to the circus.

CLOTILDE: No. I will never let you be this word again.

JOSHUA: What word?

CLOTILDE: What you said. Ringworm.

JOSHUA: Why not. I am a good ringmaster.

CLOTILDE: You are a better pirate.

JOSHUA: No, you must listen, Clotilde. You are behaving again. Like an empty head. This pirate, you are looking, he is nowhere out here. He is a poof, in your mind.

(CLOTILDE looks at JOSHUA. She looks at the audience.)

CLOTILDE: *(To audience)* I am sorry. They have deranged him. The captors. Put him in this bag and brainwashed. Emptied his mind. Like a bottle. But it is okay. I have faith. I must wait. Till the brainwash passes. And then we can let him out. He can join us again from the bag.

(CLOTILDE sits on the trapeze. She opens her parasol. She looks off into the distance. She hums a sea shanty.)

(JOSHUA regards her from the bag.)

JOSHUA: *(To audience)* I'm sorry. It is no use. She will not listen. This eyepatch, the beard, they are like a magic wand to her. All the world is changed. All the wishes, they are real. The fantasy. No logic can reach her. Nicola knows this. This Nikki Junod, she is a practical joker. All the time she makes a mockery. A travesty. Underneath she is a Jekyll and Hyde, and a couple of other people who have no business in a circus.

(CLOTILDE *hums her sea shanty.*)

(JOSHUA *watches.*)

JOSHUA: *(To audience)* Listen to her. Listen how sad. Look at her eyes resting faraway. On the horizon. I love when Clotilde's eyes can see the ocean. The high seas, can you tell? All the world, probably, every hope now, is floating before her eyes.

(CLOTILDE *stops humming.*)

CLOTILDE: Are you ready now?

JOSHUA: Pardon?

CLOTILDE: Tell me you are ready. To be my pirate again.

JOSHUA: No. I am not ready.

CLOTILDE: Then I suppose you will die lonely. In that bag.

JOSHUA: Okay. I will die lonely.

CLOTILDE: And I will die lonely too. Out here.

JOSHUA: You will die lonely?

CLOTILDE: Oh, yes. All alone.

JOSHUA: I'm sorry.

CLOTILDE: It's okay. There is no choice.

JOSHUA: No. You can go off, Clotilde.

CLOTILDE: Where? Where can I go off?

JOSHUA: You can leave me here. In this bag. I belong in a bag.

CLOTILDE: Then I will have no pirate.

JOSHUA: But what is a pirate if he is in a bag?

CLOTILDE: At least he's a pirate.

JOSHUA: No, Clotilde. This cannot be.

CLOTILDE: Yes. I would rather have a pirate. Even locked in a bag.

JOSHUA: You would stay by me? In this bag?

CLOTILDE: To the end, yes.

JOSHUA: And leave even the world?

CLOTILDE: Forever, of course.

JOSHUA: For what, Clotilde?

CLOTILDE: For my pirate. You stupid. What is the world to me without my pirate?

(JOSHUA *is moved.*)

(CLOTILDE *patiently hums.*)

JOSHUA: *(To audience)* I cannot stand this. She is impossible to resist. It is impossible to cause her to die. From loneliness like this. Perhaps if I am the pirate, just briefly this pirate, she will be happy. And I will be happy too. What harm can there be? In a little pirate?

(Pause)

JOSHUA: *(His voice changed)* Clotilde?

CLOTILDE: Hm?

JOSHUA: I am ready.

CLOTILDE: Yes?

JOSHUA: Yes, your pirate. He is here.

CLOTILDE: You have come back to me?

JOSHUA: Yes. I am back.

CLOTILDE: I knew it. I was waiting.

JOSHUA: I know. I watched you waiting.

CLOTILDE: Good. The brainwash is gone.

JOSHUA: Yes. All passed.

CLOTILDE: We must let you out of this bag.

JOSHUA: Thank you, Clotilde.

CLOTILDE: Quickly. Before the enemy comes back.

JOSHUA: The captors. I know.

(CLOTILDE *helps* JOSHUA *out of the bag.)*

CLOTILDE: Are you excited? It is exciting again to be the pirate?

JOSHUA: Oh, yes. Very excited.

CLOTILDE: Good.

JOSHUA: I am ready now to find these captors. Ready for battle.

CLOTILDE: I am ready too. They are awful, the captors.

JOSHUA: We must fight to the death with them.

CLOTILDE: We must free the high seas.

JOSHUA: And save the circus too.

CLOTILDE: Hm?

JOSHUA: We can save the circus from these captors.

CLOTILDE: What circus?

JOSHUA: The circus, Clotilde.

CLOTILDE: I do not understand this word, circus.

JOSHUA: Clotilde. We are in a circus.

CLOTILDE: No. You are a pirate now.

JOSHUA: Yes, just for you, I know. I am a pirate.

CLOTILDE: Good. Then there is no circus.

JOSHUA: *(Under his breath)* Clotilde, I did not agree to this.

CLOTILDE: *(Under her breath)* You agreed you are a pirate.

JOSHUA: Yes, but I can be a pirate in a circus.

CLOTILDE: What kind of pirate can be in a circus?

JOSHUA: A captured pirate.

CLOTILDE: No, you are gone from the bag. I have freed you.

JOSHUA: Then I'm the kind of pirate who's been called upon to save a circus.

CLOTILDE: There is no kind like that.

JOSHUA: Clotilde, I must come back and save.

CLOTILDE: *(To audience)* He is breaking my heart all over. I must die again.

JOSHUA: Clotilde, please. We must end this now. I cannot be your pirate.

CLOTILDE: *(Grasping him)* Oh, you are, you are.

JOSHUA: No, let me show you.

CLOTILDE: Don't touch. Please.

JOSHUA: I must touch. I must take this beard off.

CLOTILDE: *(Mortified)* No! You promised!

JOSHUA: *(To audience)* This is more than a man can stand. A ringmaster can have no chance against this. *(Reaching for eyepatch)* I must be brave.

CLOTILDE: No! You promised that too!

JOSHUA: Clotilde, I will keep the beard, but this eyepatch must come off. I cannot see.

CLOTILDE: Who cares for seeing?

JOSHUA: No, it cannot be. I cannot be this pirate for you. You remember the last time? When I was the pirate?

CLOTILDE: Yes. We were happy.

JOSHUA: No. It went poof.

CLOTILDE: What was poof?

JOSHUA: The happiness. It was poof.

CLOTILDE: No, we can grab it again.

JOSHUA: Clotilde, there is only emptiness under this pirate. I promise.

CLOTILDE: I don't care. You are one anyway.

JOSHUA: No. My duty is a ringmaster.

CLOTILDE: Forget about him.

JOSHUA: Clotilde, stop. You are taking advantage.

CLOTILDE: I'm sorry. I am smitten.

JOSHUA: Stop, please. Beneath this shirt you are pulling is only the chest to a ringmaster.

CLOTILDE: No, it does not have to be.

JOSHUA: Please, Clotilde. We have an audience.

CLOTILDE: Who cares about an audience?

JOSHUA: Then the circus. Clotilde, we have a circus.

CLOTILDE: Who cares for a circus?

JOSHUA: *(Weak)* I care.

CLOTILDE: No, you have lost your care.

JOSHUA: *(Weaker)* Clotilde.

CLOTILDE: All your care, it has come back to me. It is home. I am home again for the pirate.

(JOSHUA *gives up.* CLOTILDE *and* JOSHUA *embrace.)*

(*Music. Like a gentle sea shanty.)*

JOSHUA: *(His voice changed)* Clotilde?

CLOTILDE: Yes?

JOSHUA: I think I can feel him again. The pirate. He is coming back to me. In my limbs.

CLOTILDE: Good.

JOSHUA: He is happy, Clotilde. Happy to be back.

CLOTILDE: I am happy too.

JOSHUA: Faraway, yes. From the bag.

CLOTILDE: I know. You have been away so long.

JOSHUA: Yes. It has been terrible.

CLOTILDE: These captors. They are awful to dump in a bag.

JOSHUA: Terrible, I know.

CLOTILDE: To dump ashore. To brainwash. You must bring them to justice. You will do this. I know.

JOSHUA: Yes. When I find them.

CLOTILDE: You must make them to walk the plank.

JOSHUA: First, yes, I must find my ship.

CLOTILDE: You have lost your ship?

JOSHUA: They took it away. I'm sorry.

CLOTILDE: Oh, no.

JOSHUA: Also terrible storms. I was very brave. Please believe me.

CLOTILDE: Oh, I know. Of course you have been brave.

JOSHUA: But can you love me without my ship?

CLOTILDE: There is no ship to go sailing away?

JOSHUA: I am sorry.

CLOTILDE: But what can we do if we cannot sail away?

JOSHUA: Perhaps I must curl up and die.

CLOTILDE: What?

JOSHUA: I will go back, I think, to this bag.

CLOTILDE: No! I will not let you. I will stand by you.

JOSHUA: Without a ship?

CLOTILDE: I will love you, yes. Even if there is no ship. Even if the time of the pirates, it is over. Who can care?

We can stand together. Remember together this ship.
And the time of the pirate.

JOSHUA: Thank you, Clotilde.

(*The banner behind* CLOTILDE *and* JOSHUA *flutters. Then it billows.*)

(*Up above, on the pole near the high wire, a large pirate flag unfurls.*)

(*The upended wheel on the cannon begin to slowly turn, like an unattended steering wheel.*)

(*Music swells.*)

CLOTILDE: Sssh. I can hear it again.

JOSHUA: Ah, yes. It's a shanty.

CLOTILDE: You can hear the band?

JOSHUA: Yes. It is lovely.

CLOTILDE: And look. Look behind.

JOSHUA: Yes?

CLOTILDE: Look at the sail. It's billowing. (*looking up*)
Our flag too. Look. It's flapping again in the wind.

JOSHUA: What means this wind?

CLOTILDE: And can you smell? The high seas.

JOSHUA: Ah, yes.

CLOTILDE: And look. Our knees.

JOSHUA: What?

CLOTILDE: They are swaying. We have found it. We
have found the ship.

JOSHUA: We are swaying on a ship?

CLOTILDE: Yes, the captors. They fooled you.

JOSHUA: How could they fool?

CLOTILDE: They took you ashore only in your mind.

JOSHUA: No, they took me in a bag. I remember.

CLOTILDE: It was just the imagination.

JOSHUA: I cannot believe so.

CLOTILDE: Yes. They wanted to fool you. To trick you to think there was no ship. Even no high seas.

JOSHUA: I did not know this.

CLOTILDE: But look. It is the deck again. We are on deck. (*Grabbing the wheel of the cannon, as if it were a ship's wheel*) We have found the ship, where it has drifted.

JOSHUA: Clotilde, look. A bottle.

CLOTILDE: What?

JOSHUA: It is a bottle floating there.

CLOTILDE: On the ocean?

(*A DARK SHAPE has appeared, holding a long scythe. At the end of the blade is a rope from which dangles a green bottle. The bottle bobs up and down, as if on the ocean.*)

(CLOTILDE *and* CLOTILDE *watch the bottle.*)

JOSHUA: It is a message. Someone has written in a bottle. I must pick it up.

CLOTILDE: No. We must pass by.

JOSHUA: I cannot pass by. I am the captain.

CLOTILDE: No, it will have danger for you. I do not like this sight.

JOSHUA: What can have danger in a bottle?

CLOTILDE: Please. I am afraid.

JOSHUA: Don't be afraid. I am the pirate.

CLOTILDE: It's a trick, please, from the captors.

JOSHUA: No. It will tell where to find them.

CLOTILDE: Stop, please. Let another ship take the message.

JOSHUA: I cannot. My plank is hungry for these captors.

(JOSHUA *goes to the bottle and takes it off the rope. He takes a piece of paper out of the mouth of the bottle.*)

(*The* DARK SHAPE *disappears.*)

JOSHUA: (*Reading*) "Come and see me. I am waiting now across the ocean. I have a list to read to you on the other shore. Ha ha."

(*Music stops.*)

(*The banner ceases to billow. The flag falls listlessly against the pole. The cannon wheel is still.*)

JOSHUA: (*Reading*) "My name is Tooting."
(*He reaches up and lifts his eyepatch. His beard droops to one side.*)
Tooting?

(*Loud crash offstage. A dog barks. A baby cries. A whistle. Carrousel music*)

(*Enter* POLLY, LALA, WHITE HORSE *and* FLAG *from the SR wing. They are followed by the* BEAR *on a unicycle and a* DARK SHAPE *wielding a scythe. Everybody circles behind the banner and then downstage past* JOSHUA *and* CLOTILDE. *They circle back upstage. They exit back out the S R wing.*)

(*Carrousel music stops.*)

(*A balloon pops. The banner flutters.*)

CLOTILDE: I told you not to read the bottle.
(*She heads U S L.*)
Now you have lost the ship again. You have made the pirate to go poof. Because you did not listen about the bottle. You did not listen to my intuition.
(*She exits.*)

(*Pause*)

JOSHUA: *(To audience)* I am sorry. I did not know this. I did not know there could still be this pirate act in our circus.

(The distant moo of a cow is heard.)

(Several DARK SHAPES appear upstage.)

JOSHUA: *(To audience)* I promised you a parade, I know this.
I have not forgotten my promise.

(JOSHUA goes to the overturned cannon. He stuffs the beard, bandanna and eyepatch down the mouth of the cannon. He holds the green bottle. He sees NICOLA appear U S R.)

(NICOLA waves and pirouettes. She exits. The DARK SHAPES disappear.)

(Pause)

JOSHUA: *(To audience)* But we have now an intrusion of some kind. A false parade, or travesty.
Some interlopers.
And so I must track down who is in this bear. What is going on also now in the mind of our fortuneteller.

(Soft, incomplete music)

JOSHUA: And then you will see, I promise, what I meant. What is meant when I tell you our circus began in the beginning with a parade.
There was a parade.
I promised, I know, this parade.

(Music continues.)

END OF ACT ONE

ACT TWO

Escape Act

(Moments later)

*(*JOSHUA *is alone onstage.)*

JOSHUA: *(To audience)* I have a note in my hand I must explain to you. It is from the green bottle from Mr. Abaddon Tooting. And in this note he tells me, ha ha, he is waiting now across the ocean. He has a list to read on the other shore.

(Pause)

Do you see this other shore? I see no beaches here.

(He drops the green bottle down the mouth of the cannon.)

If you look also now in your program, or if you looked before, you will notice there are only eight people in our circus. Not nine. There is no Abaddon Tooting. Unless he is one of these things listed in the bottom. They are called dark shapes. Maybe beasts. So maybe Abaddon Tooting is one of these beasts. Or he is a bear. But I don't think so. Abaddon Tooting is dead. Even his name, Tooting, is from the German word "tot" which means "dead". So you can see he is not around. Unless Nicola makes some arrangements. For a hallucination to arrive on the stage. But I will guard against Nicola. And her gang of hallucinations. I will watch out for these dark shapes, for the bag they will put over me. To take me away from you.

And I will guard too against the pirate. I must not
become again the pirate.

(NICOLA *appears upstage.*)

(*The banner billows.*)

JOSHUA: (*To audience*) I must explain to you sometime, I
know, this pirate. I am sorry to behave like that.
(*He turns. He regards* NICOLA.)
Ah. Nikki.
(*Pause*)
Nicola. Are you here to present yourself again?

(*No response*)

JOSHUA: What goes on now, Nikki Junod? In the mind
these days of our fortuneteller?

NICOLA: Nothing so much.

JOSHUA: Oh?

NICOLA: Just listening. I like to listen, in moments like
this, I do. For my mother. Our Phoenician princess.

JOSHUA: Your mother is dead.

NICOLA: Oh, yes? Yes, so I've been told.

JOSHUA: You like to imagine, Nicola, that's all. This
voice of your mother. These notes also of Tooting.
(*To audience*) Her mother does not speak.

NICOLA: I'm the one who imagines, you think?
Fancy that.
Did you have fun, Josh, then? With your pirate act?
(*She regards the mouth of the cannon.*)

NICOLA: You're looking awfully stern at me, Josh.

(*Pause*)

JOSHUA: I did not know you could be this subtle. So
suggestive.

NICOLA: How do you mean, suggestive?

JOSHUA: You are always suggesting.

NICOLA: I suggest what?

JOSHUA: Yes, you know this.

NICOLA: I'm trying awfully hard, Josh. To understand what I might ever suggest.

JOSHUA: You suggested the pirate.

NICOLA: Oh?

JOSHUA: You put the beard on. A bandanna, my eyepatch.

NICOLA: Oh, those, yes. Well, I found them.

JOSHUA: You found them? Where?

NICOLA: Oh, I don't know. Lying around, I suppose. In back. I thought it was some joke. So I picked them up. Looking for a place I could dispose. But then I saw you. Resting in some sort of bag. And I thought, hmm, this must be where these belong. The bandanna, the beard, they probably fell out of this bag. And so I'll put them back. I'll give them to this man. This person sitting here in this bag.

JOSHUA: No. You knew Clotilde was coming.

NICOLA: *(Snapping)* I can't help it if you guys like to play pirate.

(Pause)

JOSHUA: No, we do not like it. How can Clotilde talk love to a pirate when there is no pirate? Or cry, look, a ship, when there is no ship?

NICOLA: Well, seemed fun.

JOSHUA: And what is the meaning of someone chasing around in a pirate flag? Like a ghost. And then also Lala and Polly. They have gone off dancing with a white horse. To a parade. Which is all in their mind.

NICOLA: Well. At least it's a parade.

JOSHUA: And where did you find that? The carrousel horse? That was lying around also? In the back?

NICOLA: I would imagine Tilgertoona-Tiglath Tily, she found it. She's the pack rat.

JOSHUA: No, Toona Tily is in the bear.

NICOLA: What bear?

JOSHUA: The bear, too, where they have gone dancing. It is Toona Tily inside that bear. Probably with a clipboard. And on this clipboard is instructions from you. To chase, I think, a pirate flag.

NICOLA: Hmm. Very dear, Joshua. These things you say, they're dear.

JOSHUA: I'm not so dear.

NICOLA: Well, paranoid, then. Perhaps it's paranoid. And I should be worried perhaps, all of us should, that our circus is being led by a man, who's taken to hiding in large canvas bags. Who talks of lost ships with a high wire mistress. Who even claims now there's a bear being trained with little notes on a clipboard. A bear who loves chasing pirate flags.
(Pause)
You should hear yourself, Joshua. You should have a good listen sometime.
(Pause)

JOSHUA: *(Quietly)* It is not paranoid to know this circus, it is not working. To know this audience, they have seen only Clotilde. She walked the wire. One little walk. Because I took advantage when she came ahead of schedule.

It is not paranoid to know this parade you have arranged, the bear, the white horse, it is mockery. Fragments. A parade only now of amputation.

(Pause)

You have told me Mr Tooting is waiting in your tent. He wishes to speak to me. Read a list.

NICOLA: Well, it's a little late, Joshua. He's gone off.

JOSHUA: Good.

NICOLA: Gone off, I believe, across the ocean. Some other shore.

JOSHUA: Uh huh. What shore is this?

NICOLA: Oh, the other side, I would say, to this world. Some place hereafter. He's eager and expecting you to join him there.

JOSHUA: No, I am happy, thank you. Right where I am.

NICOLA: Well, I don't know, Josh. Sometimes you can find yourself right on top of something before you realize it. Like that ship you sail so well.

JOSHUA: I realize only I will not look at your list from Tooting.

NICOLA: What's the matter with it?

JOSHUA: It is not real.

NICOLA: Of course it's real. I've seen it personally.

JOSHUA: It is a list to make us think the circus is over. We are hopeless. We cannot go on.

NICOLA: How could a list do that?

JOSHUA: By telling lies.

NICOLA: What lies?

JOSHUA: Everything on that list is a lie. A suggestion. A fabulation.

NICOLA: Everything?

JOSHUA: Yes, everything. I believe this. It is like a snake staring at a bird. The bird can fly away. She can have

the whole sky. But if she looks into the eyes of the
snake, if she stays to be mesmerized, then she is gone.
Gone to the belly of the beast.

(Pause)

NICOLA: Funny. Hmm. I never thought it could be a lie.
I never imagined. I thought of it as just a list.

(Pause)

Because I remember falling asleep. We had just set up
the tent. And I decided to rest a little on a bench. And
the morning was beautiful. Pristine. Just a suggestion,
that's all, of some mist. And I fell asleep, thinking, this
is good, what a day. And then I heard my mother. I
heard her call, Darling. But before I could answer, I
opened my eyes. And what I saw amazed me. Because
suddenly a strange dark wind came down from the
mountains and took up our tent. Ripped it apart. Like a
giant claw.

And I remember stepping through the wreckage, the
destruction and chaos, thinking, am I the only one here
escaped? To tell this?

But what followed was just as amazing. Because they
brought us, wounded and broken, to some town.

At which point there came an earthquake. I saw the
surrounding hillsides heave up and collapse and the
ground shift like a vast incoming wave beneath my
feet. I saw buildings break apart into pieces and vanish
like dust.

And once again I thought, am I alone here? Did I
escape alone to tell this?

At which point a fire broke out. A huge rushing fire
swept through whatever was left of us. I saw the
animals stampede, the horses escape in a panic or else
be engulfed in a fiery furnace.

And I thought, surely, the circus must end here. There
can be no circus left to go on. None of us can be left.
Surely, I only am escaped to tell this.

(Lights dim and focus on NICOLA.*)*

NICOLA: But then I heard a voice. I could not believe
I could hear these words. I could hear our ringmaster
say: We must go on. We will go on without our tent
and without the horses. No matter what influences
come to assail us. All the hounds of hell in this world,
they cannot stop us.
And I thought, does this man still retain his integrity?
Does he still believe? Like an Old Testament father?
Some blind figure from the Book of Prophets?

*(The distant sounds of wind and fire. The rumble of an
earthquake.)*

NICOLA: And I turned away, thinking, no, I want to
sleep. I will only sleep. At which point I heard my
mother again. Heard her calling across the ether. I
heard her say: Listen, Darling. Turn and listen, and you
will see a man come up like smoke from the earth, he is
coming, Darling. And so I turned.

*(She turns. She goes to the banner. She pulls it up behind her
and wraps herself in it as if it were some vast cape.)*

*(The various sheets of canvas stretched above begin to billow.
The trapeze downstage sways. The cannon wheel turns.)*

(The pirate flag above flaps furiously.)

NICOLA: I turned and felt the spirit then of my parents
rise up. I felt a wind unleashed in me. Saw my very
body erupt and heave and a fire break out and burn
through all my thoughts. I saw myself transformed.
Transfigured. And in this transfiguration I fathomed
consummation. I could tear now like a burning meteor
through all the vast night within me. And like an
ecstatic bride I turned. I saw Abaddon Tooting. I saw

Abaddon Tooting come up out of the earth. Out of the
chasm, some deep and fathomless pit, or cave. I saw
Tooting open his mouth to speak. And in his mouth
I saw water. A flood. I saw deep waters of chaos, old
night, rise up out of his mouth and swallow our earth.
I saw it wash away our people. Swallow all the sky.
And in the dark void after I saw our people were
changed. The shapes of our people had become like
thieves. Marauders. Pillaging what little was left. And
I thought, now, this is it. These thieves have come, a
flood too, and taken everything. There is nothing left.
No circus left which can go on.

*(The sounds of distant tempest and fire transform into a
crash of carrousel music.)*

NICOLA: *(Ecstatic)* It is finished.

*(The sheets of canvas above, trapeze, flag and cannon wheel
are abruptly still.)*

NICOLA: *(Blank and pitiless)* Except for me. I only will
escape alone to tell this.
(She disappears into the folds of the banner.)
(She is gone.)

The Bear Parade, part two

(Loud carrousel music continues.)

(JOSHUA is startled.)

*(Enter LALA and POLLY from the wings. POLLY wears the
left boot of a huge pair of black boots. LALA wears the right
boot of the same pair. They are dancing, holding the head of a
COW between them. Enter the PIRATE FLAG followed by the
BEAR on the unicycle. POLLY, LALA, COW, FLAG & BEAR
circle downstage.)*

*(JOSHUA recovers himself and steps forward. He trips the
FLAG which falls to the ground.)*

(Exit POLLY, LALA, COW *&* BEAR *back out the wings.)*

(Carrousel music stops.)

JOSHUA: *(To audience)* I think beneath this flag is captured Peterloo.

*(*JOSHUA *pulls off the* PIRATE FLAG. PETERLOO *lies tangled on the ground.)*

JOSHUA: Peterloo. Who told you to play ghost with a pirate flag? Did Toona Tily? Or do you take orders now from a fortuneteller?

*(*PETERLOO *looks uncomprehendingly at* JOSHUA.*)*

(More crashes of carrousel music.)

JOSHUA: Ah. They are coming again. Peterloo, we must stop this faux parade. *(Pulling her up)* We must tackle. And knock down this bear.

(Enter POLLY, LALA *and* COW *from the wings. They are fleeing from the large poster* PICTURE OF TOONA TILY.*)*

*(*PETERLOO *tugs at* JOSHUA, *pointing frantically at the* PICTURE OF TOONA TILY.*)*

JOSHUA: No, Peterloo, that is not the bear! That's not how to tackle a bear!

(The PICTURE OF TOONA TILY *collides with* PETERLOO, *who falls to the ground.)*

(The BEAR *steps out from behind the* PICTURE OF TOONA TILY. *The* BEAR *pushes* JOSHUA *into the ropes of the trapeze. The* PICTURE OF TOONA TILY *glides off into the wings.)*

(Exit POLLY, LALA *and* COW *also into the wings.)*

(Carrousel music stops.)

(The BEAR *stands over* PETERLOO. *He reaches down and takes the clown nose off* PETERLOO's *face.)*

(He opens its mouth and swallows the clown nose.)

BEAR: Grrr. Yum yum.

(Exits)

*(*JOSHUA *frees himself from the trapeze ropes. He regards* PETERLOO, *who is trying to feel where her nose was.)*

JOSHUA: *(To audience)* I think this bear costume has frightened the wits from Peterloo. *(To* PETERLOO*)* Peterloo. In this bear is only Toona Tily. Do you remember the lady? From our kissing booth?

*(*PETERLOO *looks uncomprehendingly at* JOSHUA.*)*

JOSHUA: Peterloo. We must face this bear. He is big only in your mind. He has no big mouth like a cave to swallow you. No singularity theorem to suck you away. He is only a costume.

(No response.)

JOSHUA: Peterloo. Do you remember when you came first to our circus? You wrote to me. A note which said: Excuse me, I am lost. Which way is the way to the visible world. And I said: What do you mean? We are right here. Right now in the visible world.

*(*PETERLOO *tries to remember.)*

(A faint strain of music.)

JOSHUA: And so I said: Come. I will take you. To the land of the visible world. You can be our clown.

*(*PETERLOO *touches her nose. She nods.)*

JOSHUA: And do you remember when I said there will be a new person someday?
To lead our circus?
Because in our literature, and in history, a person sometimes can take a new name. Because his travels, his experience, they have changed him to a new person. With new ideals and aims. A new perspective. Like the caterpillar who becomes the butterfly. The acorn and the oak tree. Like the phoenix who rises out of the ashes of what she was once before.

And in our circus too, it is said, someday Clotilde, her
name will become Cloisonné.
And also our child. It is said she will return. She
will come again to lead our parade. And we will not
recognize right away because she is changed.
And because she is changed, she will lead us out of
here.
And we will follow and be changed too.

(PETERLOO *is stirred. She remembers.*)

(*A burst of carrousel music.*)

JOSHUA: It's okay. We are okay now. We are ready to
tackle the bear. Bring back the circus from before.

(*Enter the* PICTURE OF TOONA TILY *from the wings.*
JOSHUA *prepares to tackle it.*)

(*Enter the* BEAR *pursuing* POLLY, LALA & COW. JOSHUA *is
confused.*)

(POLLY, LALA & COW *flee downstage.* PETERLOO *grabs
the* PICTURE OF TOONA TILY *and pushes it into their
path.* POLLY & LALA *slam into it and fall to the ground,
unconscious. The* PICTURE OF TOONA TILY *then knocks
over* PETERLOO, *who falls unconscious.*)

(*The* BEAR *pushes* JOSHUA *over the bodies of* POLLY *and*
LALA. *The* BEAR *slips behind the banner.*)

(*The* PICTURE OF TOONA TILY *glides off into the wings.*)

(*Carrousel music stops.*)

JOSHUA: (*To audience*) It is times like this I wonder
where is Clotilde. If she is in danger.

(*The* BEAR *emerges from behind the banner. He holds a
scythe with a palm tree leaf attached to the top. He plants the
handle of the scythe into the ground.*)

(*The stage darkens.*)

JOSHUA: Toona Tily?

BEAR: GRRrrr.

JOSHUA: Toona Tily!

(The sound of carrousel music)

*(*JOSHUA *scrambles to his feet. He chases the* BEAR. *They run around the banner.)*

JOSHUA: Toona Tily! Stop in that bear!

(The BEAR *and* JOSHUA *emerge again from behind the banner.)*

JOSHUA: Toona Tily! Come out of that bear!

(Exit the BEAR *into the wings. Exit* JOSHUA, *giving chase.)*

JOSHUA: *(Shouting)* Toona Tily!

(Carrousel music stops.)

(PETERLOO, POLLY *and* LALA *lie scattered and dazed, or unconscious, on the ground.)*

Mouth of the Cave

(PETERLOO *gets to her feet. She comes downstage.)*

PETERLOO: *(To audience)* While no one here can listen I want you to know about this bear I know in this bear Toona Tily is who likes to dress up or the bear Nicola Junod is even Clotilde the bear could be all are healthy suspicions but in risk of seeming lunatic I want to tell another way to view this bear because you cannot see from where I see the bear his dimensions.
I want each of you to think those occasions when this visible world isn't simply three dimensional those moments of stress when the world loses depth smashed becomes flat like a piece of paper on which is written or drawn all things we normally see except flat in this flatness is an extraordinary feeling of unreality dimensions suppressed or deja vu and the

only difference between me perhaps you is the normal
world snaps back into place you carry on whereas I
get stuck with this deja vu in front which if I look long
enough gets pushed aside or develops a rip then we
have what I call a singularity an abyss or black hole
with no color no shapes a place into which everything
can collapse all things without end like a bottomless
pit.

(Lights onstage begin to slowly dim.)

(The sound of dripping water.)

PETERLOO: I want you to think this abyss or hole as a
place has no light now the closest equivalent out here
in your visible world is a cave caves which are empty
or they house a beast throughout our literature all
history are plenty of beasts bestial presences in some
sort of cave beginning with the dragon our literature
is filled with so-called men going out to battle the
dragon Sigurd and Fafnir Saint George and the Dragon
Keresaspa and Azi Sruvara Davey Crockett even
faced beasts normally identified with living in caves
my consciousness therefore like your consciousness is
pervaded with stories certain heroes and warriors gone
forth to slay the beasts those shapes that lurk in caves
when they're not out in the countryside terrorizing the
kingdom.

I want you to think of our circus as a kingdom our
own little world once upon a time was a joyful
place to come visit we were wonderful hosts but
what happened was a beast came out from its lair to
terrorize each and all of us.

(Pause)

Now I realize there's nothing remotely frightening
about this person or thing dressed up as a bear
probably to you it seems even funny just a joke
especially when the bear attempted to change shape to

a leopard tried to get the seal off its paw and all those
balloons.

But what you see out there is different here in the
closer presence of the bear I've actually looked into
its eyes I see something blank the eyes of a sorcerer a
beast which can change shape split apart into separate
ravenous dogs I see all this bear's transparent disguise
foolish cavorting as only one of its many shapes
an effort to disarm a cloak thrown across a deeper
purpose because I see some sort of mental murder an
idolater in that bear what loves and makes a lie a great
red beast casting out a huge flood of water casting up
other shapes for us while the real dragon we're looking
to fight has become the very ground we stand on the
ground itself will swallow us like a beast coming up
out of the sea.

(One light remains on PETERLOO. *The rest of the stage is
dark.)*

PETERLOO: Anyway there's never been an appropriate
moment to bring this up.

To speak of my obsession.

I'm obsessed with this deciding whether to run or if
there's some way to battle.

And despite his limitations I admire Joshua Karabos I
do he's like an old-fashioned father to me who can wait
or expect a hired man to come who has hope and faith
when he sees the bear he thinks it's a simple matter of
tackling knocking it to the ground.

*(*DARK SHAPES *come up behind* PETERLOO.)*

PETERLOO: I love those moments when the bear seems
simple yes simple enough to tackle.

I love when I can believe when I trust yes what Joshua
says.

(The DARK SHAPES *throw a bag over* PETERLOO *and pull
her to the ground.)*

(Blackout)

(The sound of dripping continues.)

The Bear Parade, part three

"Those who cannot remember the past are condemned to repeat it."
Santayana, *The Life Of Reason*

(The sound of dripping becomes the sound of ocean waves.)

(Lights come up.)

(LALA and POLLY stand in front of the banner. They look out front.)

(LALA has the hand puppet of a SEAL on one hand. He wears the right boot of a huge pair of black boots. POLLY wears the left boot of the same pair. There is a helium balloon with the face of a LAMB tied to the hem of her dress, which lifts slightly. She absently holds a clipboard in her hands.)

(The scythe with a palm tree leaf stands to one side. A sign hangs from it.)

(Downstage is an empty canvas bag.)

(Pause)

(LALA notices POLLY.)

LALA: Do you know where this is?

POLLY: Hm?

LALA: This place. Can you tell me? This flat lonesome spot?

POLLY: I'm sorry, no, I don't know.

LALA: Hmm.
(He looks down at his hand. He tries to take the seal off. He gives up.)
I thought perhaps there could be a parade.

POLLY: Hm?

LALA: Maybe a parade. I heard about it. In the past.

POLLY: Ah.

(LALA *listens to the ocean.*)

LALA: What are we doing then? On what sounds like maybe a beach?

POLLY: I don't know.

LALA: Do you think maybe they had the parade? Which came here?

POLLY: I don't remember a parade.

LALA: Hmm. Maybe it was washed up. This parade. (*He regards the banner. He faces front again.*)

(*A distant moo is heard.*)

(POLLY *looks down at her dress. She pushes it down. It floats back up.*)

LALA: (*Puzzled*) Tell me. Was I riding one time on a big white horse with you?

POLLY: Pardon?

LALA: This is how we came here? Together on a horse?

POLLY: That's absurd.

LALA: No? Somebody else went riding with me?

POLLY: I should hope so.

LALA: Sorry if I made a mistake.

POLLY: Precisely. It take a boat.

LALA: What takes a boat?

POLLY: To come to some other shore like this. That takes a boat.

LALA: Yeah? Then how come I'm thinking all these things about you?

POLLY: What things?

LALA: Now I'm thinking of a white bunny rabbit. Did we one time talk about a bunny rabbit?

POLLY: Not that I recall.

LALA: Hmm. This woman, she looked just like you.

POLLY: You've tangled me, mentally. With some other woman.

LALA: Yeah? Okay, then how about the bear? I know I have seen you one time with a bear.

POLLY: I think you're a lunatic.

LALA: You must be British.

POLLY: Pardon?

LALA: The British, they like to forget all these things. Whatever can lurk. In the libido.

POLLY: My libido's perfectly fine, thank you.

LALA: Then how come we wear the same boot?

POLLY: Boot, you say?

LALA: Down there, it's the same boot. Do you think it could be a case of reincarnation? You and me?

POLLY: Never, no.

LALA: Yeah, I think so. I think I chase you from life to life trying to remind you.

POLLY: Do you normally approach people like this? Utter strangers. With this sort of conversation?

LALA: I'm just asking about reincarnation.

POLLY: You should be ashamed of yourself. Reincarnation. Using an old ploy like that. An old man making passes at a frisky person like myself. On the basis of reincarnation.

LALA: You're not so frisky. I happen to be very frisky.

POLLY: *(Pushing down her dress)* Would you mind not doing that?

LALA: I have lots of cavorting left in me.

POLLY: Would mind not lifting my dress?

LALA: I'm not lifting. I have hands nowhere near to your dress.

POLLY: You have something on that hand, by the way.

LALA: Yeah, I know. It doesn't come off.

POLLY: On your shirt too.

LALA: Hm?

POLLY: It's sticking out. A piece of paper.

LALA: Yeah. Looks like somebody left a note.

POLLY: Oh, dear. I have one too.

LALA: No kidding?

POLLY: A note, yes. On a clipboard.

LALA: We should read them. They can tell us why we are here.

POLLY: You think so?

LALA: Yeah. Could be like a fortune cookie.

POLLY: Very well.

(LALA and POLLY open their pieces of paper.)

LALA: What does it say, your note?

POLLY: Hmm. *(Reading)* "Come and see me. I am waiting now across the ocean. I have a list to read to you on the other shore."

LALA: Yeah? My note, it says: "Ha ha. My name is Tooting."
Who is Tooting?

POLLY: Never heard of him.

LALA: *(Looking down at his boot)* No, I think I heard one time about a Tooting.

POLLY: Look. Over there. It's a sign.

LALA: Oh, yeah, a sign?

POLLY: Yes, somebody's left it. On a tropical tree.

LALA: Maybe this Tooting. He left a sign.
(He approaches the sign.)
(Reading) "Those who cannot remember the past, ha ha, are condemned to repeat it."

(A distant moo is heard.)

POLLY: Rather silly for a sign, don't you think? It even presupposes to point somewhere.

(Enter a BEAR from the direction the sign is pointing. The BEAR is much larger than before and walks on all four legs. He slowly circles downstage past LALA and POLLY. He circles back upstage. He comes to a halt. He stands there, teetering.)

(LALA and POLLY regard the BEAR.)

LALA: I told you there was a bear. We are condemned now to repeat this bear.

(The BEAR falls to the ground. It lies there.)

LALA: What's he doing, this bear? He's supposed to roar. Then haul off and chase me.

POLLY: I hear they're unpredictable. Perhaps he's still hibernating.

LALA: Yeah, he's tricky, this bear. I remember.

POLLY: How on earth did he get here?

LALA: Maybe he came the same way which we came.

POLLY: What, on a horse?

LALA: Yeah, or could be a boat. He could have swum the whole way across the ocean.

POLLY: Oh, dear.

(The stage begins to darken. DARK SHAPES *appear and disappear. The banner billows.)*

(The sound of ocean waves gathers force.)

(Enter NICOLA *upstage. She regards* LALA *and* POLLY. *They do not notice.)*

POLLY: Perhaps we better sneak off, then. Head inland. Before he wakes up.

LALA: Yeah. We better fly right out of here.

*(*LALA *and* POLLY *quickly exit, each slipping or stumbling out of the pair of huge black boots.)*

(The ocean waves continue.)

Eye of the Carrousel

(The stage becomes calm.)

*(*NICOLA *regards the sleeping* BEAR *and discarded boots.)*

NICOLA: *(To audience)* You're probably wondering by now, yes? Where is Tilgertoona-Tiglath Tily? We have not been seeing Toona Tily. Is she down in there? In this bear? Or is she maybe in back, I wonder. Chasing after Peterloo?

(The stage darkens.)

NICOLA: She's endearing, don't you think? Toona Tily. She takes such big marching steps. Or tiptoe steps. Like a choo-choo train. And she's tiny in those clothes she wears. This is enchanting to people. They want to give her a kiss. Even my mother, I remember, and the man she adored, even Tooting, found Toona Tily quite pleasing.
How could one dislike?
Such innocence.

She is like Clotilde, I think. A child living in the body
of a woman. That part of us which will never grow up.
No matter what claims to have happened to us. When
we were little.

(Soft strains of music. NICOLA regards the high wire.)

NICOLA: I remember watching Clotilde one time.
Walking up there. Like an angel. And I thought, what
on earth is it like in the mind of Clotilde when she
walks up there? What thoughts must she have?

(Something discordant seeps into the music.)

(DARK SHAPES appear and disappear.)

*(NICOLA goes to the canvas bag lying onstage. She takes a
small jar from the mouth of the bag. She opens the jar. She
applies whiteface.)*

NICOLA: And I thought of that word "angel." What she
makes me think of. And another word which I found
came to mind. The word "fallen."
And then I noticed that line Clotilde walked on.
This thin, dark thing dividing the firmament. And I
thought, just a passing thought, what if Clotilde could
look down? And have a thought, or perceive perhaps
a snake. If that line up there could curl and lift itself up
and speak to her. Take a deep look in her eyes.
*(Her face is covered with whiteface. She takes an eyebrow
pencil and lip rouge out of the mouth of the bag. She applies
them to herself.)*
Those were my thoughts. These words I heard.
Which I suggested to her. Quietly, when she came
down. I told her of my premonition. I forewarned she
could fall. Take a terrible tumble, Darling.
So I suggested she be careful. Oh, so very careful up
there.

And then I took care to let her know, that if she should indeed ever fall, she would be saved. Because there was a pirate man who would come.
She would be saved someday by this pirate.
(She takes a top hat and overcoat out of the canvas bag. She steps into the pair of big black boots. She puts on the overcoat. She dons the top hat.)

(It is TOONA TILY.*)*

TOONA TILY: *(To audience)* Pretty hat. Pretty girl in a hat. Kitty cat. GRRrrr. No touching.

*(*TOONA TILY *marches upstage. The sound of marching boots.)*

TOONA TILY: Parade! *(To audience)* Yum yum.

*(*TOONA TILY *joins the* DARK SHAPES *upstage. They disappear.)*

(Sound of boots fades.)

(The BEAR *begins to shake and heave.)*

The Last Pirate Act

(The sound of ocean waves returns.)

(The BEAR *sits up. It shakes its head vigorously. The head falls off.)*

(It is JOSHUA.*)*

JOSHUA: *(To himself)* I am in a bag again?
(He looks about. He sees his paw.)
I am a bear?

*(*JOSHUA *sees the* BEAR's *head on the ground.)*

JOSHUA: No. I have been captured. This time in a bear. These captors, they have no bounds.

(JOSHUA attempts to stand. The back half of the BEAR *remains on the ground.)*

JOSHUA: What's happening to me in this bear?

(JOSHUA feels around in the BEAR.*)*

JOSHUA: *(With horror)* I have a partner in this bear.

(JOSHUA struggles inside the BEAR.*)*

JOSHUA: *(Sternly)* Toona Tily? Are you inside this bear?

(The head of PETERLOO *pops out through the folds of the* BEAR.*)*

JOSHUA: *(Astonished)* Peterloo. What are you doing with me in this bear?
Is this the way, you think? To tackle a bear?

(PETERLOO looks blankly at JOSHUA.*)*

(JOSHUA regards the empty stage.)

JOSHUA: *(Confused)* How can I be a bear now? Which I chased?

(PETERLOO disappears back into the folds of the BEAR. *The back half of the* BEAR *rolls and struggles.)*

JOSHUA: Peterloo, no ,wait! What are you fighting down there in the bear?
Peterloo!

(DARK SHAPES appear. They force the head of the BEAR *back over* JOSHUA. *They drag both halves of the* BEAR *upstage. They roll the* BEAR *behind the banner.)*

(Enter CLOTILDE *from a wing.)*

(She comes cautiously downstage.)

CLOTILDE: *(To audience)* They say I am an empty head. It is not so. I am waiting only to hear something. Because I have heard two voices in my life. And when they spoke. My life was changed.

(Lights dim and focus on CLOTILDE.*)*

CLOTILDE: The first voice I heard was a fortuneteller. I cannot remember this lady. I would like to. Very much. Because when she spoke it was like a wind across my face. A fire in my mind, and my feet, I could feel them tremble. But she told me I would not remember her face. And I said: No, how can I forget such a face? I will remember. I will be faithful. But she said: No, you will forget. And it is true. I have forgotten. I remember only words. She told me I will be saved someday by a pirate. And I am very grateful she told this fortune. I did not know before.

(Pause)

The second voice was when I fell from a great height. And I lay down to sleep in a dark cave. And in my sleep I saw a great ocean and no one who could come to me. Until I heard the voice of someone coming ashore. He called out. He fought his way to make me hear. And then I knew, this is the pirate. He is come from beyond the horizon. Together we will go face the Great Captor. We will meet on the high seas. To do battle. We will even cast our bodies against him. Because my body is nothing to me. Without my pirate.

(Music. The approach of an ethereal parade.)

CLOTILDE: Oh. There is one last voice I must tell. Because I went marching one time. On a long line which was stretched across the sky. I do not remember the knowledge I had. To march like that across the air and all the earth. But I remember a voice. The kindest I have ever heard. The most strong and still. It kept me safe. It played for me a strange and wonderful sound. I saw the mountains and hills. They were singing. I saw trees clapping their hands. And then I saw my feet. The feet of a child. They were beautiful. And so I asked the voice which kept me safe, I said: Tell me the name of these feet. They are beautiful. And then I heard the name, Cloisonné. And I said: Who is that? And then I

heard: You are Cloisonné. I will call you that, and you
will know it is me. You will know I have sent someone,
Cloisonné. To lead you out of here.

(Music stops.)

CLOTILDE: Of all the voices I have heard, if it speaks
again, I will follow.
Even if I must leave behind the pirate. Go faraway
from him.

(She sits on the trapeze. She waits.)

(The sound of ocean waves returns.)

(Lights come up.)

*(Enter the BEAR from behind the banner. The front half
of the BEAR is dragging the back half which appears to be
empty. The BEAR lurches across the stage, blind. It comes to
a stop. It shakes it head vigorously. The head falls off.)*

(It is JOSHUA.)

JOSHUA: Peterloo?

*(JOSHUA climbs out of the BEAR. He looks back down the
neck of the BEAR.)*

JOSHUA: Peterloo?

(CLOTILDE continues to gaze out to sea.)

*(JOSHUA pulls out a sword, a floppy hat, eyepatch and
bandanna from the body of the BEAR. He looks at them and
tosses them aside. He pulls out the head of a WHITE HORSE
on the end of a carrousel pole. He puts it aside. He pulls out
a parasol.)*

JOSHUA: Clotilde?

(JOSHUA turns and sees CLOTILDE sitting on the trapeze.)

JOSHUA: I am chasing a bear all the time for Clotilde?
(Going to CLOTILDE) Clotilde! I am so happy to find you
again. To see you safe and sound.

(CLOTILDE *continues to gaze out to sea.*)

JOSHUA: Clotilde? Hello, Clotilde?

(JOSHUA *looks out to sea. He looks back at* CLOTILDE.)

JOSHUA: *(Realizing)* Ah. She is gazing now out to sea. I must come to her, quick, from across the ocean.

(JOSHUA *places the parasol in* CLOTILDE'*s lap. He goes back to the empty* BEAR. *He retrieves the bandanna, eyepatch, floppy hat and sword. He puts them on.*)

(*He regards the* WHITE HORSE *and* CLOTILDE *on the trapeze.*)

JOSHUA: Will she think a pirate must ride a horse when he comes to land?

(JOSHUA *decides to straddle the* WHITE HORSE.)

JOSHUA: *(Pleased)* I hope I'm not too dashing on this horse.

(JOSHUA *rides the* WHITE HORSE *over to* CLOTILDE. *Soft music.*)

JOSHUA: Hello. How are you today?

CLOTILDE: *(Vaguely)* Who are you?

JOSHUA: I am the pirate. I have come back.

CLOTILDE: Oh?

JOSHUA: You do not recognize me?

CLOTILDE: No, sorry. I do not think so.

JOSHUA: How can this be?

CLOTILDE: My pirate does not arrive on a horse. He has a ship.

JOSHUA: He has a horse too.

CLOTILDE: Ah.

JOSHUA: He has a ship for the ocean and a horse for the land.

CLOTILDE: I did not know this.

JOSHUA: I can get off the horse if it will please you.

CLOTILDE: I would recognize my pirate. Even on a horse.

JOSHUA: How can you not recognize? You always recognize.

CLOTILDE: Because you do not look like a pirate to me. You are too rinkydink.

(Music peters out.)

JOSHUA: Something is wrong. *(Checking himself)* Floppy hat, an eyepatch, one sword, big bandanna.

CLOTILDE: You don't have a beard.

JOSHUA: Pardon?

CLOTILDE: I know a pirate with a beard.

JOSHUA: That is correct. He has a beard.

CLOTILDE: You are no pirate.

JOSHUA: I know. I'm sorry.

CLOTILDE: You could be killed pretending like this.

JOSHUA: Excuse me. I must go back now and get this pirate. I will send him out to you.
(He rides back to the banner.)

CLOTILDE: *(To audience)* Always my pirate does this. He tries to trick me. He sends a rinkydink first, to test if I am faithful.

(JOSHUA dismounts and looks inside the BEAR. He finds the beard and puts it on. He tosses aside the WHITE HORSE and strides boldly back to CLOTILDE.)

JOSHUA: *(His voice changed)* Okay. I am back. I am the pirate.

CLOTILDE: I know. I can tell.

JOSHUA: Good. I am glad.

CLOTILDE: There was a man here before. He tried to tell me he was you.

JOSHUA: I know. I saw him.

CLOTILDE: But I sent him away. I was faithful.

JOSHUA: I have been faithful too.

CLOTILDE: Did you bring our ship?

JOSHUA: Hm?

CLOTILDE: They took our ship again? The captors?

JOSHUA: No. It was a bear.

CLOTILDE: Pardon?

JOSHUA: I fought my way back from the belly of a bear.

CLOTILDE: Ah. I see they have deranged you again.

JOSHUA: Who deranged?

CLOTILDE: All the time. These captors.

JOSHUA: Never.

CLOTILDE: Yes. Last time it was the poof bottle.

JOSHUA: What bottle?

CLOTILDE: The poof bottle. You stupid.

JOSHUA: Ah, yes.

CLOTILDE: This bear, he is only a new bag. A new trick to take you ashore in your mind. But we must not believe anymore these tricks. We will throw them overboard!

(CLOTILDE *picks up the* BEAR *costume. She drags it off into the wings. A loud splash is heard. She tosses the* WHITE HORSE *into the wings. Another splash*)

CLOTILDE: This tree too! I throw it overboard!

(She pulls up the scythe with a palm tree leaf. She tosses it into the wings.)

(Loud splash)

CLOTILDE: Good! They are all overboard. All the brainwash is gone!

(The banner flutters. Then it billows.)

(Up above, on the pole near the high wire, the large pirate flag unfurls.)

(Music. It swells.)

CLOTILDE: Yes! We are happy again!

JOSHUA: I am happy now?

CLOTILDE: Yes, it is our ship! You don't see it?

JOSHUA: Where? Where is our ship?

CLOTILDE: All around. Right here. Look. Our knees.

JOSHUA: My knees are shaking?

CLOTILDE: No, they are swaying. And look. Behind. Look at the sail. It's billowing. Our flag too. It is flapping again in the wind.

JOSHUA: We have found our ship?

CLOTILDE: Yes, it was drifting. But now we are aboard again!

(A loud boom is heard.)

(The trapeze sways. The sheets of canvas above fill with wind.)

(The sound of an ocean storm.)

JOSHUA: What is this?

CLOTILDE: It is the Great Captor. We are in his lair.

JOSHUA: I did not see this Captor coming.

CLOTILDE: Quick. Our cannon.

JOSHUA: Pardon?

CLOTILDE: We must answer with our cannon.

JOSHUA: Ah, yes.

(Another loud boom.)

*(*CLOTILDE *and* JOSHUA *rush toward the overturned cannon. They right it and push it into position.)*

JOSHUA: Where is he? This Chief Captor?

CLOTILDE: He has surrounded our ship. We must shoot.
(She lights the cannon. Nothing)
(She sticks her hand into the nozzle.)

JOSHUA: Clotilde!

*(*CLOTILDE *pulls out a large black boot.)*

CLOTILDE: What is this? Who has put a boot in our cannon?

JOSHUA: *(Taking it)* Toona Tily? Nikki Junod?

(A large hissing sound. Then a growl. The wind howls.)

CLOTILDE: Look!

JOSHUA: What?

CLOTILDE: It is something out there! It is coming now from the ocean!

JOSHUA: I cannot tell what it is.

CLOTILDE: It is a leopard!

JOSHUA: No, how can there be a leopard on an ocean?

CLOTILDE: Then a bear!

JOSHUA: No. No, it is no bear. It has too many heads.

CLOTILDE: Where is the ship?

JOSHUA: What?

CLOTILDE: We have lost the ship.

JOSHUA: You can see no ship?

(The various sheets stretched in the air above, and the banner itself, have become filled with the images of predatory BEASTS *and* DARK SHAPES.*)*

*(*JOSHUA *and* CLOTILDE *turn to each other.)*

CLOTILDE: My pirate.

JOSHUA: Yes, Clotilde?

CLOTILDE: I am afraid.

JOSHUA: Don't be afraid. I am here.

CLOTILDE: No, they will take you away. I will be lost.

JOSHUA: Who will take me?

CLOTILDE: I will be all alone again.

JOSHUA: *(Defiant)* Who will take this man of your dreams!?

(The BEASTS *and* DARK SHAPES *approach and change and combine until finally a huge* FIGURE, *holding a scythe, looms up and fills the whole banner. The* FIGURE's *scythe comes crashing down on* JOSHUA.*)*

(A terrible scraping sound. CLOTILDE *screams.)*

(Blackout)

(The sound of an ocean storm recedes.)

(The sound of a carrousel)

(Lights come up on various DARK SHAPES *and the figures of* LALA, POLLY *and* JOSHUA, *who still wears a pirate hat and beard. They each hold the head of an* ANIMAL, *or* BEAST, *at the end of a long pole. The poles move up and down like a carrousel as they circle the stage. In the center is* TOONA TILY, *wearing an oversized top hat and one big boot. She waves to the audience with the paw of a* BEAR. *The other hand holds aloft a scythe.)*

TOONA TILY: *(To audience)* Parade, yum yum. Goody, GRRrrr. No touching.

(Blackout)

(The sound of a carrousel continues.)

The Beginning of the Parade

(Soft lights come up on CLOTILDE.*)*

(She drifts past the banner. She picks up a broken balloon off the floor. She sees a CARROUSEL HORSE *lying on the ground. She goes to pick it up. She starts to wander offstage with it.)*

(The sound of an instrument quietly playing.)

*(*CLOTILDE *turns and notices the silhouette of someone sitting off to the side.)*

(It is PASQUALE.*)*

(Pause)

PASQUALE: *(Gently)* Are you leaving?

CLOTILDE: Hm?

PASQUALE: Where are you going?

CLOTILDE: I found a horse.

PASQUALE: Yes?

CLOTILDE: I thought I would ride. I thought he would take me someplace. Take me away.
He's pretty, don't you think, my horse?

(No response)

*(*PASQUALE *remains sitting, a dark outline, on the side.)*

CLOTILDE: Who are you?

PASQUALE: I was told there was a circus.

CLOTILDE: *(Putting aside the* CARROUSEL HORSE*)* What circus?

PASQUALE: I have come here. To work in a circus.

CLOTILDE: No, it is not here. We have no circus.

PASQUALE: Oh?

CLOTILDE: Yes, perhaps you must look somewhere else. If there was a circus, it is gone. I'm sorry.

PASQUALE: No, I think I'll take a look here.

CLOTILDE: Why? There is nothing to look.

PASQUALE: That's not what I heard.

CLOTILDE: Okay. Good luck to you then.

PASQUALE: Thank you.

CLOTILDE: I hope you find what you are looking for.

(CLOTILDE *starts to wander off again toward the* CARROUSEL HORSE. *She stops.)*

CLOTILDE: Who told you there was a circus?

PASQUALE: You don't see it?

CLOTILDE: Do I see what?

PASQUALE: A circus.

CLOTILDE: Where? Where is a circus?

PASQUALE: All around. Right here.

CLOTILDE: You see a circus all around?

PASQUALE: Everywhere, yes.

CLOTILDE: You are a funny person.

PASQUALE: No, I'm serious.

CLOTILDE: Then why cannot I see this circus? What is in it, the circus?

PASQUALE: Many animals, actually. All kinds of people. They are gathering right now. For a parade.

CLOTILDE: Really? A parade?

PASQUALE: The most beautiful parade, yes.

CLOTILDE: Uh huh. I cannot see this parade.

PASQUALE: You are not looking.

CLOTILDE: No, I am. I am looking very hard.

PASQUALE: Then what do you see?

CLOTILDE: I see nothing. What do you see?

PASQUALE: I see on all sides a parade. It is waiting for us.

CLOTILDE: They are waiting?

PASQUALE: Yes, they won't go on without us. They are waiting for us to see them. So we can join.

CLOTILDE: You can see all this?

PASQUALE: Oh, yes. Very clearly.

(CLOTILDE *regards the empty stage.*)

CLOTILDE: I am sorry. I must have missed this parade. They are gone by.
(Pause)
I have seen you before?

PASQUALE: Yes.

CLOTILDE: You were a child before?

PASQUALE: Yes.

CLOTILDE: And where have you been? Since you were a child?

PASQUALE: I went on ahead.

CLOTILDE: Pardon?

PASQUALE: I was told to go ahead.

CLOTILDE: Oh. I don't remember.

(PASQUALE *stands. She approaches* CLOTILDE.)

(*She is* PETERLOO. *What was once* PETERLOO *is now* PASQUALE.)

PASQUALE: I went on ahead, because I was told there
was a beast. I must go to him. Find the place where
he lives. And so I left, went off alone, to find this
beast. I searched every possible place I could think up
ahead. Every visible world. Until I lost all bearing, all
memory, and I wandered, like a vagabond, to a land
of no mountains, no trees, and nothing alive. Where
the wind of other planets blew across the ground. And
in this land I found a dark place where a beast could
live. A beast which spoke to me. He said: Where is
your circus? And I answered: It is coming behind. They
will be here soon. And he said: Do you know there has
been some calamity? A great wind? And I answered:
No, I did not know. And then he said: There was an
earthquake too. Even a fire. And after the fire, great
delusions have broken out among your people. They
no longer recognize, or remember, who they are. They
are warlike instead. Thieves. And I said: No, I did not
know any of these things. And so he said: Then what
is it you do know? And I said: I have been sent ahead.
I was told to meet you here. To which he answered:
You are late then. It is too late. All these things have
happened. It is finished. While you wandered like a
vagabond.
(Pause)
And when he said that, I turned and saw a great wind
tearing at the mouth of the place where he lived.
Pushing over mountains and rocks. And I thought I
must call on that wind. To help me. But then I saw
the wind was his. It belonged to him. And then I felt
the whole ground move, and I thought to call on
the earthquake to destroy this beast. But I saw the
earthquake was his too. And the same with the fire.
The fire wasn't mine to call.

And so I asked. I said: What is here for me to call?
And then I heard a still small voice. And in this voice I
heard: He's lying. He loves and makes a lie.
And when the beast saw what I heard, he opened his
mouth wide, and out of his mouth came a flood of
water to wash away this voice I heard. A whole ocean.
But I just stepped, or was lifted like a bird. I saw the
place he lived vanish like nothing in the air. And then
I saw all the mountains were in place. I saw trees
and great rivers. I saw a bear and a cow, they played
together. Leopards and lions, they were all friendly to
me. And as I walked along, I could hear him cursing
and shouting after me: What if they do not believe
you! What if they will tell you themselves that all these
things have happened! They will tell you they have
seen them!
So I turned back to the cave. But all I could see was a
small dark hole. Which was turning, as it disappeared
into a great expanse of clear air. And I called out to it.
I answered: They will choose not to believe you. You
have no power at all. To prevent what they choose.

(PASQUALE *goes to* CLOTILDE. *She takes the* CARROUSEL
HORSE *and puts it aside.*)

PASQUALE: They are waiting for us.

CLOTILDE: Hm?

PASQUALE: The parade. They are waiting for us to lead.
You and I.

CLOTILDE: I will lead the parade with you?

PASQUALE: Yes, you will walk with us. In the air.

CLOTILDE: I will walk in the air?

PASQUALE: Up above, yes.

(CLOTILDE *looks up at the high wire.*)

PASQUALE: What do you see there, Cloisonné?

CLOTILDE: Hm?

PASQUALE: Tell me.

CLOTILDE: I don't know. I can't tell.

PASQUALE: Take a look.

CLOTILDE: It's a snake?

PASQUALE: *(Gently)* No. No, it's not a snake, Cloisonné.

(Pause)

CLOTILDE: *(Realizing)* I went marching one time. Sometime ago.

PASQUALE: That's right.

(Soft, incomplete music)

CLOTILDE: What sound is that?

PASQUALE: It is the parade.

CLOTILDE: A parade is coming?

PASQUALE: Yes. You will see it soon.

CLOTILDE: Good. I am happy to see a parade.

PASQUALE: Climb up then.

CLOTILDE: I must climb?

PASQUALE: Yes, they are waiting.

CLOTILDE: Okay. Okay, I am coming.

(Lights dim, except for a light on CLOTILDE *as she climbs the pole up to the high wire. She pauses halfway up.)*

(Another light comes up JOSHUA. *He comes downstage.)*

(The music continues.)

JOSHUA: *(To audience)* Pretty still, yes? This stillness for a circus?
Hardly even any music.
(He listens.)

(To audience) There should be a parade right now.
Don't you think?
(He turns. He sees CLOTILDE.*)*
How do you do, Clotilde?

CLOTILDE: I am fine.

JOSHUA: Good.

CLOTILDE: Very fine. Thank you.

JOSHUA: How's the music today? Do you hear music?

CLOTILDE: Pardon?

JOSHUA: *(To audience)* She hears music. A band in her head.

CLOTILDE: Joshua?

JOSHUA: Hm?

CLOTILDE: I have a message for you.

JOSHUA: A message? Yes, Clotilde.

CLOTILDE: You must take this message to the pirate.

JOSHUA: The pirate, okay. What shall I tell the pirate?

CLOTILDE: Tell him I will be away. For a long time. He must forget about me.

JOSHUA: Yes? He must forget?

CLOTILDE: It is no use. Tell him.

JOSHUA: Okay. I will tell him.

CLOTILDE: Thank you.

JOSHUA: He will be very sad.

CLOTILDE: Why?

JOSHUA: Because he was close to you, this pirate.

CLOTILDE: Joshua?

JOSHUA: Yes?

CLOTILDE: You are a wonderful pirate.

JOSHUA: Hm?

CLOTILDE: I will always remember you were a wonderful pirate. I will remember how you helped a little girl.

JOSHUA: What little girl?

CLOTILDE: I was like a little girl. When we spoke together like that and you were the pirate.

JOSHUA: *(Moved)* Ah. Thank you. Cloisonné.

CLOTILDE: *(To audience)* You must listen to this man. This man, he is our ringmaster now.

(Another light comes up on NICOLA. *She is sitting on the ground, holding the* CARROUSEL HORSE. *She strokes it, trying to bring it back to life. Her face still has traces of whiteface, and one hand is still the paw of a* BEAR.)

JOSHUA: Nicola?
Nikki Junod?

*(*NICOLA *looks about herself in great fear. She gets up from the ground, clinging to the* CARROUSEL HORSE.)

JOSHUA: Nicola Junod, what are you doing?

CLOTILDE: Sssh.

JOSHUA: What?

CLOTILDE: She cannot see you.

JOSHUA: No? What does she see?

CLOTILDE: She sees a beast.

JOSHUA: What beast?

CLOTILDE: She was told there was a beast. She told us to expect it. It was coming.

(Pause)

JOSHUA: I don't see a beast.

CLOTILDE: No. He is gone.

JOSHUA: What was this beast going to do to us?

CLOTILDE: I think it meant to frighten.

JOSHUA: Ah.

CLOTILDE: Go to her.

JOSHUA: Hm?

CLOTILDE: Go to Nicola. She is in trouble. She can still see a beast.

(JOSHUA *goes to* NICOLA. *She cowers before him. He reaches out and takes her by the hand. She loses sight of him and cowers away from something else.*)

(JOSHUA *leads her downstage. She remains unaware of him.*)

JOSHUA: *(To audience)* And so. Welcome back to our circus. We are a circus again. We are all back now.

(JOSHUA *regards* NICOLA, *who continues to cling to the* CARROUSEL HORSE.)

(CLOTILDE, *meanwhile, climbs to the top of the pole.*)

JOSHUA: *(To audience)* We have lost our fortuneteller. I'm sorry. She has been captured in her mind by a beast. A beast which hoped to go from there and to cover the whole circus. Like a veil. And perhaps Nicola thought she could lead maybe because of this beast. She could train it. But he turned on her. And so she is very frightened.
But we will care for her. Because this beast, he will someday let her go. We know this. He can only stay so long in there, in the mind of Nicola.
Because we are out here. To stay by her. To keep her company. We will take her along. Until she has realized. Until she can see she has joined us again too.

(Music. The approach of an ethereal parade)

JOSHUA: *(Smiling broadly)* And now. What I have always promised for you. What I have always known,

or heard, I should promise. Our parade. The beginning
of our parade. Which is here. It has always been here.
Like a promise. For us to fulfill.

(A sound like mountains, or rivers, filling with music.)

(Enter PASQUALE *leading a small* CHILD *by the hand.)*

(Up above, enter CLOTILDE, *walking on wire.)*

(Enter POLLY *and* LALA. *Enter other jugglers and acrobats.)*

*(*JOSHUA *stands by, proudly watching. He holds* NICOLA *by
the hand.)*

*(The various canvas sheets in the air above the stage, and
the banner itself, begin to fill with images of many people
across the world, and all sorts of living creatures, all moving
forward in one infinite parade.)*

END OF PLAY

www.ingramcontent.com/pod-product-compliance
Lightning Source LLC
Chambersburg PA
CBHW052153090426
42741CB00010B/2257